CAMBRIDGE SCHOOL

Shakespeare

The Merry Wives of Windsor

Edited by Rex Gibson

Series Editor: Rex Gibson
Director, Shakespeare and Schools Project

CAMBRIDGE
UNIVERSITY PRESS

CAMBRIDGE UNIVERSITY PRESS
Cambridge, New York, Melbourne, Madrid, Cape Town,
Singapore, São Paulo, Delhi, Mexico City

Cambridge University Press
The Edinburgh Building, Cambridge CB2 8RU, UK

www.cambridge.org
Information on this title: www.cambridge.org/9780521000550

First published 2003
4th printing 2013

Printed and bound in the United Kingdom by the MPG Books Group

A catalogue record for this publication is available from the British Library

ISBN 978-0-521-00055-0 Paperback

Prepared for publication by Stenton Associates
Designed by Richard Morris, Stonesfield Design

Thanks are due to the following for permission to reproduce photographs:

Cover image: from the 1985 RSC production in Stratford, with (left) Janet Dale as Meg Page and (right) Lindsay Duncan as Alice Ford, directed by Bill Alexander, designed by William Dudley. Photo credit: Donald Cooper/Photostage, England. 12, 26, 33, 40, 50, 67, 98, 105, 118, 134, 138, 159, 171, 187 Donald Cooper/Photostage; 84, 150 Angus McBean; 167 Royal Shakespeare Theatre, Stratford-upon-Avon; 177 Shakespeare Centre Library, Nobby Clark; 183 Victoria and Albert Museum, London.

Contents

Cambridge School Shakespeare

This edition of *The Merry Wives of Windsor* is part of the *Cambridge School Shakespeare* series. Like every other play in the series, it has been specially prepared to help all students in schools and colleges.

This *Merry Wives of Windsor* aims to be different from other editions of the play. It invites you to bring the play to life in your classroom, hall or drama studio through enjoyable activities that will increase your understanding. Actors have created their different versions of the play over the centuries. Similarly, you are encouraged to make up your own mind about *The Merry Wives of Windsor*, rather than having someone else's interpretation handed down to you.

Cambridge School Shakespeare does not offer you a cut-down or simplified version of the play. This is Shakespeare's language, filled with imaginative possibilities. You will find on every left-hand page: a summary of the action, an explanation of unfamiliar words, and a choice of activities on Shakespeare's language, characters and stories.

Between each act and in the pages at the end of the play, you will find notes, illustrations and activities. These will help to increase your understanding of the whole play.

There are a large number of activities to give you the widest choice to suit your own particular needs. Please don't think you have to do every one. Choose the activities that help you most.

This edition will be of value to you whether you are studying for an examination, reading for pleasure, or thinking of putting on the play to entertain others. You can work on the activities on your own or in groups. Many of the activities suggest a particular group size, but don't be afraid to make up smaller or larger groups to suit your own purposes.

Although you are invited to treat *The Merry Wives of Windsor* as a play, you don't need special dramatic or theatrical skills to do the activities. By choosing your activities, and by exploring and experimenting, you can make your own interpretations of Shakespeare's language, characters and stories. Whatever you do, remember that Shakespeare wrote his plays to be acted, watched and enjoyed.

Rex Gibson

This edition of *The Merry Wives of Windsor* uses the text of the play established by David Crane in *The New Cambridge Shakespeare*.

List of characters

Citizens of Windsor

MISTRESS ALICE FORD
MASTER FRANK FORD her husband
JOHN and ROBERT their servants

MISTRESS MARGARET PAGE
MASTER GEORGE PAGE her husband
ANNE PAGE (Nan) their daughter
WILLIAM PAGE their son

DOCTOR CAIUS a French doctor, suitor to Anne Page
MISTRESS QUICKLY his housekeeper
JOHN RUGBY his servant
SIR HUGH EVANS a Welsh parson and schoolteacher
THE HOST of the Garter Inn

Children of Windsor who appear in the last act as fairies.

Visitors to Windsor

SIR JOHN FALSTAFF
ROBIN his page
BARDOLPH, PISTOL, NIM } his followers

MASTER FENTON a young gentleman in love with Anne Page

MASTER ROBERT SHALLOW a country justice
MASTER ABRAHAM SLENDER his nephew, suitor to Anne Page
PETER SIMPLE servant to Slender

The action of the play takes place in Windsor.

Shallow intends to prosecute Falstaff. Shallow claims high status as a gentleman and is strongly supported by Slender. Sir Hugh Evans offers to make peace between Shallow and Falstaff.

---

1 Getting started (in pairs or small groups)

How would you stage the opening moments of the play? In some productions, the entire cast has appeared, each character bustling about, creating the busy life of Elizabethan Windsor. In others, only the three named characters appear, with Shallow virtually exploding with rage as he expresses his indignation against Falstaff. Talk together about each of the following, then work out how you would stage the opening moments to greatest dramatic effect.

a Shakespeare immediately provides clues to how preoccupied characters are with their social status. The first word spoken is 'Sir', but that was a courtesy title for a clergyman with a university degree (Sir Hugh Evans' social standing is not equal to Sir John Falstaff's). Shallow insists he is an 'Esquire', a rank one degree below a knight. He stresses his importance as a gentleman entitled to a coat of arms. Although his social status is lower than Falstaff's, he seems determined to take the fat knight to court (you will discover why as you read on).

b An Elizabethan audience would recognise Shallow and Slender as foolish characters in the way that both of them, boasting about Shallow's high status, show their ignorance of Latin words.

c Shakespeare provides clues in Sir Hugh Evans' language that he is going to be a comic stereotype of a Welsh clergyman and schoolteacher. He mistakes 'luces' for 'louses' (because he thinks 'luce' is the singular of 'lice'), and he uses 'py' for 'by' ('py'r Lady' = 'by our Lady'). In performance, actors use a strong Welsh accent and rhythms of speech.

Star Chamber royal court (its ceiling was decorated with stars)
Coram (quorum) a specially important justice of the peace
Custalorum Shallow mangles *Custos Rotulorum* (Latin: chief justice of a county)
Ratolorum Slender also mangles the Latin!
Armigero (armiger) a gentleman entitled to a coat of arms
passant heraldic term for walking
quarter heraldic term for adding a coat of arms to one's own

The Merry Wives of Windsor

Act 1 Scene 1
Outside Master Page's house

Enter JUSTICE SHALLOW, SLENDER, and SIR HUGH EVANS

SHALLOW Sir Hugh, persuade me not. I will make a Star Chamber matter of it. If he were twenty Sir John Falstaffs, he shall not abuse Robert Shallow, Esquire.

SLENDER In the county of Gloucester, Justice of Peace and Coram.

SHALLOW Ay, cousin Slender, and Custalorum.

SLENDER Ay, and Ratolorum too; and a gentleman born, Master Parson, who writes himself Armigero in any bill, warrant, quittance, or obligation – Armigero.

SHALLOW Ay, that I do, and have done any time these three hundred years.

SLENDER All his successors gone before him hath done't, and all his ancestors that come after him may. They may give the dozen white luces in their coat.

SHALLOW It is an old coat.

EVANS The dozen white louses do become an old coat well. It agrees well passant. It is a familiar beast to man, and signifies love.

SHALLOW The luce is the fresh fish. The salt fish is an old coat.

SLENDER I may quarter, coz.

SHALLOW You may, by marrying.

EVANS It is marring indeed, if he quarter it.

SHALLOW Not a whit.

EVANS Yes, py'r Lady. If he has a quarter of your coat there is but three skirts for yourself, in my simple conjectures. But that is all one. If Sir John Falstaff have committed disparagements unto you, I am of the Church, and will be glad to do my benevolence to make atonements and compromises between you.

Shallow continues to threaten to take action against Falstaff, but Evans' talk of Slender marrying the rich heiress Anne Page finally distracts him. The three men greet Master Page.

---

1 A comic Welshman? (in pairs)

Shallow threatens that the Council (the king's court) shall hear (try) the charge of rioting he intends to bring against Falstaff. Sir Hugh Evans mistakes his words, thinking that the court will actually hear the riot. Shakespeare gives Evans the language of the comic stage Welshman who says 'Got' for 'God', 'petter' for 'better'.

Talk together about whether you think the humour is entirely acceptable in the context of the play or whether Evans' style of speaking is offensive to Welsh people.

2 Points of view (in groups of three)

Evans suggests that Slender ('Master Abraham') marry Anne Page. The three men discuss Anne's appearance and financial prospects: she will inherit much wealth from her grandfather and father. Take parts and read aloud lines 33–48. Then one person steps into role as a feminist critic, another as a Marxist critic. In role as critic, each gives their response to the episode.

- Feminist critics express women's points of view (what might Anne Page say about the men's discussion of her?).
- Marxist critics argue that money and power is at the root of all human relationships.

3 'It was ill killed'

Shallow has sent venison (deer meat) to Page, but says it was 'ill killed'. He may mean that the deer was clumsily and illegally killed by Falstaff. Check line 87 to see if that is a plausible interpretation.

Council the King's Council
Take your visaments think carefully
the sword should end it I would challenge him to a duel
petter that friends is the sword friendship is better than fighting
device idea, plan
grandsire grandfather
goot motion good idea
pribbles and prabbles bickering and squabbling
possibilities financial prospects
peradventures perhaps

SHALLOW The Council shall hear it; it is a riot.

EVANS It is not meet the Council hear a riot. There is no fear of Got in a riot. The Council, look you, shall desire to hear the fear of Got, and not to hear a riot. Take your visaments in that.

SHALLOW Ha! O'my life, if I were young again, the sword should end it.

EVANS It is petter that friends is the sword, and end it. And there is also another device in my prain, which peradventure prings goot discretions with it. There is Anne Page, which is daughter to Master George Page, which is pretty virginity.

SLENDER Mistress Anne Page? She has brown hair, and speaks small like a woman.

EVANS It is that fery person for all the 'orld, as just as you will desire. And seven hundred pounds of moneys, and gold, and silver, is her grandsire upon his death's-bed (Got deliver to a joyful resurrections!) give, when she is able to overtake seventeen years old. It were a goot motion if we leave our pribbles and prabbles, and desire a marriage between Master Abraham and Mistress Anne Page.

SLENDER Did her grandsire leave her seven hundred pound?

EVANS Ay, and her father is make her a petter penny.

SHALLOW I know the young gentlewoman. She has good gifts.

EVANS Seven hundred pounds, and possibilities, is goot gifts.

SHALLOW Well, let us see honest Master Page. Is Falstaff there?

EVANS Shall I tell you a lie? I do despise a liar as I do despise one that is false, or as I despise one that is not true. The knight Sir John is there; and I beseech you be ruled by your well-willers. I will peat the door for Master Page. [*He knocks*] What ho! Got pless your house here!

[*Enter* PAGE]

PAGE Who's there?

EVANS Here is Got's plessing and your friend, and Justice Shallow, and here young Master Slender, that peradventures shall tell you another tale, if matters grow to your likings.

PAGE I am glad to see your worships well. I thank you for my venison, Master Shallow.

SHALLOW Master Page, I am glad to see you. Much good do it your good heart! I wished your venison better; it was ill killed. How doth good Mistress Page? And I thank you always with my heart, la, with my heart.

Shallow rebukes Slender for criticising Page's hunting dog. Falstaff cheerfully admits that he assaulted Shallow's men, killed his deer, and broke Slender's head. He refuses to be serious and mocks Shallow.

1 Elizabethan England: Shakespeare's England

The play takes place in the time of King Henry V (probably around 1413), but it constantly evokes the world of Queen Elizabeth I around the time the play was written (late 1590s). For example, Slender refers to the Elizabethan 'sport' of hare coursing on the Cotswold hills ('Cotsall'). Page's greyhound was outrun by another dog, and failed to catch the hare it chased.

Page is not pleased to be reminded of his dog's poor performance, but Slender teases him, repeating 'You'll not confess'. Shallow tries to shut him up, probably worried that Slender might be upsetting his prospective father-in-law. He repeatedly insists that Page's dog is 'good and fair' (technical terms for hunting dogs).

As you read on you will find many more examples of how the play reflects life in Shakespeare's England (see especially pages 161–2).

2 Enter Sir John Falstaff (in pairs)

Falstaff immediately reveals his mocking style:

Line 89: He jokingly adds to Shallow's list of complaints.

Lines 91–5: He twists the meaning of words: Shallow says his complaints must be 'answered' (in court), Falstaff replies he will 'answer' here and now; Shallow declares the king's 'Council' shall know of his wrongs, Falstaff responds that they were better 'known in counsel' (kept private).

Line 97: He mimics Evans' accent.

Advise Falstaff on how to deliver each of his five speeches opposite.

---

fallow light brown
do a good office make peace
confessed admitted
redressed punished, put right
the King Henry V (reigned 1413–1422)
lodge hunting lodge
Tut, a pin! What nonsense!
Pauca verba few words (don't go on)
worts Evans' Welsh pronunciation of 'words'; cabbage-type plants
matter complaint

PAGE Sir, I thank you.

SHALLOW Sir, I thank you; by yea and no I do.

PAGE I am glad to see you, good Master Slender.

SLENDER How does your fallow greyhound, sir? I heard say he was outrun on Cotsall.

PAGE It could not be judged, sir.

SLENDER You'll not confess, you'll not confess.

SHALLOW That he will not. [*Aside to Slender*] 'Tis your fault, 'tis your fault. [*To Page*] 'Tis a good dog.

PAGE A cur, sir.

SHALLOW Sir, he's a good dog and a fair dog. Can there be more said? He is good and fair. Is Sir John Falstaff here?

PAGE Sir, he is within; and I would I could do a good office between you.

EVANS It is spoke as a Christians ought to speak.

SHALLOW He hath wronged me, Master Page.

PAGE Sir, he doth in some sort confess it.

SHALLOW If it be confessed, it is not redressed. Is not that so, Master Page? He hath wronged me, indeed he hath, at a word he hath. Believe me. Robert Shallow, Esquire, saith he is wronged.

[*Enter* SIR JOHN FALSTAFF, PISTOL, BARDOLPH, *and* NIM]

PAGE Here comes Sir John.

FALSTAFF Now, Master Shallow, you'll complain of me to the King?

SHALLOW Knight, you have beaten my men, killed my deer, and broke open my lodge.

FALSTAFF But not kissed your keeper's daughter?

SHALLOW Tut, a pin! This shall be answered.

FALSTAFF I will answer it straight. I have done all this. That is now answered.

SHALLOW The Council shall know this.

FALSTAFF 'Twere better for you if it were known in counsel. You'll be laughed at.

EVANS *Pauca verba*, Sir John, good worts.

FALSTAFF Good worts? Good cabbage! Slender, I broke your head. What matter have you against me?

Slender claims he has been robbed by Falstaff's followers. They threaten him. In a parody of a trial, Pistol denies Slender's accusations and Nim again threatens him. Slender accuses Bardolph.

---

1 Focus on Slender (in groups of seven)

The dispute between Shallow and Falstaff now disappears entirely from the play, and is replaced by an episode (lines 99–149) in which Slender's accusations result in a mock trial. He calls Pistol, Nim and Bardolph swindling tricksters ('cony' = rabbit). Take parts and rehearse the lines using the following to help you:

Lines 99-108: The three men respond to Slender's accusation with insults and threats that obviously intimidate him: 'Banbury cheese' = pale and thin; 'Mephostophilus' = devil; 'Slice' = cut (Nim may finger his knife meaningfully).

Lines 109–15: Evans proposes to have the case judged by himself, Page and the host of the Garter. He pompously uses '*fidelicet*', his Welsh pronunciation of the Latin videlicet = 'namely'.

Lines 116–38: Falstaff takes over! Slender lists what he has lost, but Pistol, using exaggerated and theatrical language throws the accusation back in his teeth. Nim threatens violence if Slender presses the charges ('marry, trap!' was a cry in a children's game), so Slender accuses Bardolph, whose red nose reminds Falstaff of Robin Hood's 'merry men': Will Scarlet and Little John.

2 Slender: an appropriate name

Slender is easily intimidated. He responds to Bardolph's and Pistol's insults with 'Ay, it is no matter', and to Nim's threat by calling for his servant Simple. He tries to pluck up courage, swearing three times 'by these gloves', and then 'By this hat'. His name is a clue to his personality (an activity about characters' names is on page 66).

---

matter ideas, injuries
humour fancy (see pages 22, 40)
tam mother (dam)
groats, millsixpences coins
Edward shovel-boards coin of Edward VI used in pub game
Yed Edward
mountain-foreigner Welsh hill-dweller
latten bilbo tin sword (puny like Slender)
labras lips (Latin)
run the nuthook's humour behave like a constable

SLENDER Marry, sir, I have matter in my head against you, and against your cony-catching rascals, Bardolph, Nim, and Pistol. They carried me to the tavern and made me drunk, and afterward picked my pocket.

BARDOLPH You Banbury cheese!

SLENDER Ay, it is no matter.

PISTOL How now, Mephostophilus?

SLENDER Ay, it is no matter.

NIM Slice, I say. *Pauca, pauca.* Slice, that's my humour.

SLENDER Where's Simple, my man? Can you tell, cousin?

EVANS Peace, I pray you. Now let us understand. There is three umpires in this matter, as I understand: that is, Master Page (*fidelicet* Master Page); and there is myself (*fidelicet* myself); and the three party is (lastly and finally) mine host of the Garter.

PAGE We three to hear it, and end it between them.

EVANS Fery goot. I will make a prief of it in my notebook, and we will afterwards 'ork upon the cause with as great discreetly as we can.

FALSTAFF Pistol!

PISTOL He hears with ears.

EVANS The tevil and his tam! What phrase is this? 'He hears with ears'?
Why, it is affectations.

FALSTAFF Pistol, did you pick Master Slender's purse?

SLENDER Ay, by these gloves did he, or I would I might never come in mine own great chamber again else, of seven groats in mill-sixpences, and two Edward shovel-boards that cost me two shilling and twopence apiece of Yed Miller, by these gloves.

FALSTAFF Is this true, Pistol?

EVANS No, it is false, if it is a pickpurse.

PISTOL Ha, thou mountain-foreigner! Sir John and master mine,
I combat challenge of this latten bilbo!
Word of denial in thy *labras* here!
Word of denial! Froth and scum, thou liest!

SLENDER [*Pointing to Nim*] By these gloves, then 'twas he.

NIM Be advised, sir, and pass good humours. I will say 'marry, trap!' with you, if you run the nuthook's humour on me; that is the very note of it.

SLENDER By this hat, then he in the red face had it. For though I cannot remember what I did when you made me drunk, yet I am not altogether an ass.

FALSTAFF What say you, Scarlet and John?

Bardolph claims that Slender was drunk and thrown out of the tavern. Falstaff judges the disputes ended. Slender is overwhelmed by the sight of Anne Page, but misunderstands Shallow's talk of marriage.

1 Deliberately misleading? (in pairs)

Bardolph, like other characters in the play, mangles or uses obscure language. He uses 'sentences' for 'senses', 'fap' for 'drunk', 'cashiered' for 'thrown out' (or 'lost his cash') and 'careers' for 'rapid gallop'. He quite defeats Slender who thinks he must be talking Latin.

But is Bardolph being deliberately obscure? Talk together about whether you think his intention is mainly to baffle Slender.

2 Why are they silent? (in small groups)

Anne Page and Mistress Ford and Mistress Page enter, but Shakespeare gives them no language. Take turns to give your response to each of the following questions:

a Why does Shakespeare keep the women silent?

b How might Anne Page behave in her brief, one-line appearance?

c How does each man on stage respond to the sight of Anne?

d Why does Falstaff kiss only Mistress Ford?

e How might the two Wives behave during their time on stage?

Remember, there is no single 'right' answer to any question, but your responses should always have dramatic effect in mind.

3 Learning to love

Slender wishes he had his book of *Songs and Sonnets*: a very popular collection of poems published in 1557 and known as *Tottel's Miscellany*. Slender thinks its love poems can help him woo Anne Page. But his thoughts quickly turn to the *Book of Riddles*, a 'joke' book. What does that suggest to you about Slender's nature?

---

conclusions passed the careers events happened in a mad gallop
by my troth in truth
drink down all unkindness drown all disputes in friendly drinking
Allhallowmas All Saints' Day, 1 November
Michaelmas 29 September (Simple muddles the dates)
coz cousin (loosely used by Elizabethans for family relationship)
tender proposal

BARDOLPH Why sir, for my part, I say the gentleman had drunk himself out of his five sentences.

EVANS It is 'his five senses'. Fie, what the ignorance is!

BARDOLPH And being fap, sir, was, as they say, cashiered; and so conclusions passed the careers.

SLENDER Ay, you spake in Latin then too. But 'tis no matter. I'll ne'er be drunk whilst I live again but in honest, civil, godly company, for this trick. If I be drunk, I'll be drunk with those that have the fear of God, and not with drunken knaves.

EVANS So Got 'udge me, that is a virtuous mind.

FALSTAFF You hear all these matters denied, gentlemen. You hear it.

[*Enter* ANNE PAGE *with wine*]

PAGE Nay, daughter, carry the wine in; we'll drink within.

[*Exit Anne Page*]

SLENDER O heaven, this is Mistress Anne Page!

[*Enter* MISTRESS FORD *and* MISTRESS PAGE]

PAGE How now, Mistress Ford?

FALSTAFF Mistress Ford, by my troth, you are very well met. By your leave, good mistress.

[*He kisses her*]

PAGE Wife, bid these gentlemen welcome. Come, we have a hot venison pasty to dinner. Come, gentlemen, I hope we shall drink down all unkindness.

[*Exeunt all except Slender, Shallow, and Evans*]

SLENDER I had rather than forty shillings I had my book of *Songs and Sonnets* here.

[*Enter* SIMPLE]

How now, Simple, where have you been? I must wait on myself, must I? You have not the *Book of Riddles* about you, have you?

SIMPLE *Book of Riddles*? Why, did you not lend it to Alice Shortcake upon Allhallowmas last, a fortnight afore Michaelmas?

SHALLOW Come, coz; come, coz; we stay for you. A word with you, coz. Marry, this, coz: there is, as 'twere, a tender, a kind of tender, made afar off by Sir Hugh here. Do you understand me?

SLENDER Ay, sir, you shall find me reasonable. If it be so, I shall do that that is reason.

It takes Slender some time to understand that Shallow and Evans are talking about his marrying Anne, rather than about his grievances against Pistol, Nim and Bardolph. His responses show his dim-wittedness.

From left to right: Shallow, Slender and Evans. Slender's language becomes increasingly muddled. He says the opposite of what he intends, hoping heaven will 'decrease' his love for Anne (he means 'increase'), that their familiarity will breed 'contempt' (content), and that he is 'dissolved, and dissolutely' (resolved, and resolutely) to marry Anne. Which line opposite do you think is being spoken at this moment?

motions words, proposal
point main thing (sexual innuendo = penis)
divers various
good will sincere feelings (or sexual desire)
possitable positively
desires feelings (or sexual desire)
conceive understand (or beget a child)
pleasure please (or give sexual satisfaction)
fall mistake

SHALLOW Nay, but understand me.

SLENDER So I do, sir.

EVANS Give ear to his motions. Master Slender, I will description the matter to you, if you be capacity of it.

SLENDER Nay, I will do as my cousin Shallow says. I pray you pardon me. He's a justice of peace in his country, simple though I stand here.

EVANS But that is not the question. The question is concerning your marriage.

SHALLOW Ay, there's the point, sir.

EVANS Marry is it; the very point of it – to Mistress Anne Page.

SLENDER Why, if it be so, I will marry her upon any reasonable demands.

EVANS But can you affection the 'oman? Let us command to know that of your mouth, or of your lips; for divers philosophers hold that the lips is parcel of the mouth. Therefore precisely, can you carry your good will to the maid?

SHALLOW Cousin Abraham Slender, can you love her?

SLENDER I hope, sir, I will do as it shall become one that would do reason.

EVANS Nay, Got's lords and his ladies, you must speak possitable, if you can carry her your desires towards her.

SHALLOW That you must. Will you, upon good dowry, marry her?

SLENDER I will do a greater thing than that upon your request, cousin, in any reason.

SHALLOW Nay, conceive me, conceive me, sweet coz; what I do is to pleasure you, coz. Can you love the maid?

SLENDER I will marry her, sir, at your request; but if there be no great love in the beginning, yet heaven may decrease it upon better acquaintance, when we are married and have more occasion to know one another. I hope upon familiarity will grow more contempt. But if you say 'marry her', I will marry her; that I am freely dissolved, and dissolutely.

EVANS It is a fery discretion answer, save the fall is in the 'ord 'dissolutely'. The 'ort is, according to our meaning, 'resolutely'. His meaning is good.

SHALLOW Ay, I think my cousin meant well.

SLENDER Ay, or else I would I might be hanged, la!

Anne Page brings her father's request that the men come in and dine. Shallow and Evans accept, but Slender declines. Alone with Anne, Slender displays great awkwardness in conversation.

---

1 Elizabethan England (in pairs)

Slender's uneasy conversation with Anne displays his gaucheness, but it also contains rich reminders of Shakespeare's England. Take parts as Slender and Anne and speak lines 213–39 to bring out Slender's lack of social skills as he tries to talk about things that probably either embarrass or bore Anne.

Line 217: It was considered socially inappropriate for a man to bring his own servants to his host's house.

Line 219: Wealthy young Elizabethan men had three or four servants, and Slender callously looks ahead to having more when his mother dies. Inheritance was a major preoccupation of Elizabethans.

Lines 225–6: Practising sword-fencing was a popular pastime, and many professional 'master[s] of fence' (fencing teachers) ran schools to teach fencing skills to rich young men.

Lines 227–8: 'stewed prunes' and 'hot meat' were slang terms for a prostitute. Slender seems to imply he fenced three bouts ('veneys') for a whore as a prize.

Lines 228-39: Bear-baiting, in which dogs were set upon a chained bear, was a popular 'sport' in Elizabethan England. A bear-baiting ring stood close to Shakespeare's Globe theatre on London's Bankside. The site is still called Bear Gardens. Sackerson was a famous bear who was tormented there. Slender's enthusiasm for the 'sport' is unmistakable ('That's meat and drink to me'), but Anne may be revolted by his enjoyment.

Would I were young for your sake (Shallow is flattering Anne on her beauty)

'Od's plessèd will God's blessed will

quarrel at it pick a fight with another spectator at the bear-baiting (Slender is trying to create a macho image)

gentle gentleman (Page may be beginning to think of Slender as a future high-status son-in-law)

[*Enter* ANNE PAGE]

SHALLOW Here comes fair Mistress Anne. Would I were young for your sake, Mistress Anne.

ANNE The dinner is on the table. My father desires your worships' company.

SHALLOW I will wait on him, fair Mistress Anne.

EVANS 'Od's plessèd will! I will not be absence at the grace.

[*Exeunt Shallow and Evans*]

ANNE Will't please your worship to come in, sir?

SLENDER No, I thank you, forsooth, heartily; I am very well.

ANNE The dinner attends you, sir.

SLENDER I am not a-hungry, I thank you, forsooth. [*To Simple*] Go, sirrah, for all you are my man, go wait upon my cousin Shallow.

[*Exit Simple*]

A justice of peace sometime may be beholding to his friend for a man. I keep but three men and a boy yet, till my mother be dead. But what though? Yet I live like a poor gentleman born.

ANNE I may not go in without your worship; they will not sit till you come.

SLENDER I'faith, I'll eat nothing; I thank you as much as though I did.

ANNE I pray you, sir, walk in.

SLENDER I had rather walk here, I thank you. I bruised my shin the other day with playing at sword and dagger with a master of fence – three veneys for a dish of stewed prunes – and, by my troth, I cannot abide the smell of hot meat since. Why do your dogs bark so? Be there bears i'th'town?

ANNE I think there are, sir; I heard them talked of.

SLENDER I love the sport well, but I shall as soon quarrel at it as any man in England. You are afraid if you see the bear loose, are you not?

ANNE Ay, indeed, sir.

SLENDER That's meat and drink to me, now. I have seen Sackerson loose, twenty times, and have taken him by the chain. But I warrant you, the women have so cried and shrieked at it that it passed. But women, indeed, cannot abide 'em; they are very ill-favoured rough things.

[*Enter* PAGE]

PAGE Come, gentle Master Slender, come; we stay for you.

SLENDER I'll eat nothing, I thank you, sir.

Slender insists that Page and Anne precede him into the house, but finally enters first. In Scene 2, Evans sends Simple to Mistress Quickly with a letter asking her to help Slender's wooing of Anne.

---

1 More awkwardness (in groups of three)

Slender has just made a mess of talking with Anne. Now he shows a similar lack of social skills as he tries to be courteous about who should enter the house first. Talk together about how Page and Anne might behave to their awkward guest, then work out a performance of lines 240–51 to greatest comic effect.

2 'By cock and pie'

Page's expression is a mild oath. 'Cock' stands for 'God' and 'pie' refers to the Catholic church service. But in Shakespeare's day these original meanings, dating from medieval times, had been lost, and the oath caused no offence. The Elizabethan authorities disapproved of 'God' being spoken on stage and plays were often censored, with the word being removed. But Evans the Welshman gets away with blasphemy, because of the way he pronounces 'God'. Glance back through Scene 1 and count how many times Evans avoids censorship by speaking 'God' as 'Got' or ''Od's'.

3 Act it out (in pairs)

Take turns to speak as Evans and Simple and read Scene 2 aloud. Your main task is to show how Evans might speak. You may not feel comfortable mimicking the Welshman, but just for the purposes of this activity, put aside your worries about mocking stereotypes and don't be afraid to go over the top. For example, Evans might smack his lips at line 10, because, according to stereotype, Welshmen were great lovers of cheese.

After you have both practised speaking as Evans, talk together about your feelings about creating a 'stage Welshman'.

---

nurse … dry nurse housekeeper (Evans may prissily want to make it clear that Mistress Quickly is not a 'wet nurse', a woman who breast-feeds a child)

his laundry, his washer, and his wringer Evans typically spells out at length that Mistress Quickly does Doctor Caius' washing

altogethers acquaintance closely acquainted

pippins apples

PAGE By cock and pie, you shall not choose, sir. Come, come.

SLENDER Nay, pray you lead the way.

PAGE Come on, sir.

SLENDER Mistress Anne, yourself shall go first.

ANNE Not I, sir. Pray you, keep on.

SLENDER Truly, I will not go first, truly, la! I will not do you that wrong.

ANNE I pray you, sir.

SLENDER [*Going first*] I'll rather be unmannerly than troublesome. You do yourself wrong, indeed, la!

Exeunt

Act 1 Scene 2
Sir Hugh Evans' house

Enter EVANS and SIMPLE

EVANS Go your ways, and ask of Doctor Caius' house which is the way. And there dwells one Mistress Quickly, which is in the manner of his nurse, or his dry nurse, or his cook, or his laundry, his washer, and his wringer.

SIMPLE Well, sir.

EVANS Nay, it is petter yet. Give her this letter, for it is a 'oman that is altogethers acquaintance with Mistress Anne Page, and the letter is to desire and require her to solicit your master's desires to Mistress Anne Page. I pray you be gone. I will make an end of my dinner; there's pippins and cheese to come.

Exeunt

Falstaff says he must get rid of some of his followers. The Host of the Garter employs Bardolph as barman. Falstaff, nearly penniless, declares he must cheat someone: he has Ford in mind.

1 Strange characters! (in small groups)

The Host of the Garter: The jovial landlord of Windsor's Garter Inn has his own distinctive style of speaking. He calls other characters 'bully', a term that means something like 'brave fellow' or 'good companion'. He uses exaggerated comparisons, flattering Falstaff as 'Hercules' (the strongest man), 'Hector' (Trojan hero), and piling up descriptions of him as 'emperor': 'Caesar, Kaiser, and Pheazar' (the last word is probably from 'vizier').

Bardolph and Nim: Falstaff seems relieved to be rid of Bardolph, describing him as a 'tinderbox' (red-nosed and explosive) and an unskilful thief. Pistol is disgusted that Bardolph has become a barman ('spigot' means beer-tap), but Nim (who is obsessed by the word 'humour') makes a joke of it, saying Bardolph's parents were drunk when they conceived him.

Pistol: Pistol uses exaggerated language, extreme and theatrically melodramatic, as if he is half-remembering old tragedies he had seen on stage. He uses old-fashioned words rarely heard in Shakespeare's time: 'ken' (know) and 'wight' (man).

a Practise ways of speaking the Host's lines that express his genial, confident style.

b Take turns to speak all Pistol says opposite, and fit actions to his words as you feel appropriate. For example, 'fico' (fig, or sexual intercourse) was usually accompanied with an obscene gesture.

---

cashier, wag, trot dismiss
sit at ten pounds a week (Falstaff's expenses at the Garter)
draw, tap act as barman
froth and lime cheat customers by putting a frothy head on beer and lime in sour wine
gotten conceived
humour fancy
minute's rest minim rest, a pause in music
kibes chilblains
cony-catch swindle (literally, trap rabbits)

Act 1 Scene 3
The Garter Inn

Enter FALSTAFF, HOST, BARDOLPH, NIM, PISTOL, and ROBIN

FALSTAFF Mine host of the Garter!

HOST What says my bully rook? Speak scholarly and wisely.

FALSTAFF Truly, mine host, I must turn away some of my followers.

HOST Discard, bully Hercules, cashier. Let them wag; trot, trot.

FALSTAFF I sit at ten pounds a week.

HOST Thou'rt an emperor: Caesar, Kaiser, and Pheazar. I will entertain Bardolph; he shall draw, he shall tap. Said I well, bully Hector?

FALSTAFF Do so, good mine host.

HOST I have spoke. Let him follow. [*To Bardolph*] Let me see thee froth and lime. I am at a word. Follow.

[*Exit*]

FALSTAFF Bardolph, follow him. A tapster is a good trade. An old cloak makes a new jerkin; a withered servingman a fresh tapster. Go, adieu.

BARDOLPH It is a life that I have desired. I will thrive.

[*Exit*]

PISTOL O base Hungarian wight, wilt thou the spigot wield?

NIM He was gotten in drink. Is not the humour conceited?

FALSTAFF I am glad I am so acquit of this tinderbox. His thefts were too open. His filching was like an unskilful singer, he kept not time.

NIM The good humour is to steal at a minute's rest.

PISTOL 'Convey', the wise it call. 'Steal'? Foh, a fico for the phrase!

FALSTAFF Well, sirs, I am almost out at heels.

PISTOL Why then, let kibes ensue.

FALSTAFF There is no remedy: I must cony-catch; I must shift.

PISTOL Young ravens must have food.

FALSTAFF Which of you know Ford of this town?

PISTOL I ken the wight. He is of substance good.

FALSTAFF My honest lads, I will tell you what I am about.

PISTOL Two yards and more.

Falstaff reveals his plot. He will make love to Mistress Ford and Mistress Page and steal their money. Pistol and Nim indignantly refuse to deliver Falstaff's letters to the women, so he dismisses them.

---

1 Appearance and reality: fooling himself? (in pairs)

Falstaff seems convinced that the two Wives wish to have an affair with him. He claims Mistress Ford gave him 'the leer of invitation' ('come hither' looks), and that Mistress Page also sexily eyed him up ('most judicious œillades'). Identify the three sections opposite where Falstaff claims the women desperately fancy him, and say whether you think he is telling the truth or just fantasising.

2 Images of wealth

Falstaff wants to get his hands on the money! He declares that both wives have control of their husbands' wealth, and he uses vivid imagery drawn from Elizabethan England to describe it.

Line 39: His pun means both 'an army of angels' and 'a host of gold coins' (an angel was an Elizabethan coin).

Line 51: Guiana was believed to contain El Dorado (golden city), the object of Sir Walter Raleigh's 1595 voyage.

Lines 51–2: 'Cheaters' were escheaters, Elizabethan officials who collected taxes for the exchequer (and a popular pun on 'cheat').

Line 53: The East and West Indies were seen as places of fabulous wealth, ripe for exploitation by Elizabethan explorers.

Which of the above images might prompt Falstaff's line 61?

3 Why? (in pairs)

Talk together about why Pistol and Nim refuse to carry the letters, and why Falstaff dismisses them.

---

carves carves meat for guests
construe interpret, translate
hardest voice deepest meaning
will desire (probably sexual)
The anchor is deep Falstaff firmly believes it!
humour see pages 22, 40
burning-glass magnifying glass
Pandarus go-between, pimp
Lucifer the Devil
pinnace small boat
French thrift servants dismissed in hard times.
skirted fashionably dressed

FALSTAFF No quips now, Pistol. Indeed I am in the waist two yards about, but I am now about no waste; I am about thrift. Briefly, I do mean to make love to Ford's wife. I spy entertainment in her. She discourses, she carves, she gives the leer of invitation. I can construe the action of her familiar style; and the hardest voice of her behaviour, to be Englished rightly, is 'I am Sir John Falstaff's'.

PISTOL He hath studied her will, and translated her will – out of honesty into English.

NIM The anchor is deep. Will that humour pass?

FALSTAFF Now, the report goes she has all the rule of her husband's purse; he hath a legion of angels.

PISTOL As many devils entertain, and 'To her, boy!', say I.

NIM The humour rises; it is good. Humour me the angels.

FALSTAFF [*Showing letters*] I have writ me here a letter to her; and here another to Page's wife, who even now gave me good eyes too, examined my parts with most judicious œillades. Sometimes the beam of her view gilded my foot, sometimes my portly belly.

PISTOL Then did the sun on dunghill shine.

NIM I thank thee for that humour.

FALSTAFF O, she did so course o'er my exteriors, with such a greedy intention, that the appetite of her eye did seem to scorch me up like a burning-glass. Here's another letter to her. She bears the purse too. She is a region in Guiana, all gold and bounty. I will be cheaters to them both, and they shall be exchequers to me. They shall be my East and West Indies, and I will trade to them both. [*To Nim*] Go, bear thou this letter to Mistress Page; [*To Pistol*] and thou this to Mistress Ford. We will thrive, lads, we will thrive.

PISTOL Shall I Sir Pandarus of Troy become,
And by my side wear steel? Then Lucifer take all!

[*He gives back the letter*]

NIM I will run no base humour. Here, take the humour-letter. [*He gives it back*] I will keep the haviour of reputation.

FALSTAFF [*To Robin*] Hold, sirrah, bear you these letters tightly;
Sail like my pinnace to these golden shores.
Rogues, hence, avaunt! Vanish like hailstones, go!
Trudge, plod away o'th'hoof, seek shelter, pack!
Falstaff will learn the humour of the age:
French thrift, you rogues – myself and skirted page.

[*Exeunt Falstaff and Robin*]

Pistol and Nim, angered by their dismissal, plan their revenge. They will reveal Falstaff's love plots to the husbands. In Scene 4, Mistress Quickly warns of Doctor Caius' quirkiness with visitors and language.

---

1 Cunning plans (in pairs)

Pistol's 'For gourd and fulham holds' means nothing to a modern audience, but would have been understood by Elizabethans. 'Gourd and fulham' were loaded dice, and Shakespeare's audience would know that Pistol now intends trickery. He makes it even clearer in his next line (67): cunning deceives everyone.

The two men's revenge plan is to tell the husbands that Falstaff intends to seduce their wives. Pistol's lines 74–7 are in strongly rhyming and rhythmical verse. Try speaking the lines aloud several times, then talk together about whether you feel that, in performance, Pistol should or should not exaggerate the rhymes and rhythm.

2 'That is my true humour' (in pairs)

Nim has a fixation about the word 'humour'. He uses it obsessively. In Nim's constant use, Shakespeare may be satirising the fact that the word had become very fashionable in the 1590s. He shows that in Nim's constant repetition, it becomes almost meaningless.

Identify every time Nim uses 'humour' in Scene 3. Suggest what he might mean by each. Remember that often, he himself probably doesn't know!

3 'Mars of malcontents'

Pistol's comparison of Nim to Mars, the Roman god of war, refers to a fashionable pose adopted in Shakespeare's time. The malcontent was a familiar figure, in real life and in theatre. He railed bitterly against society, and was like 'the angry young man' of the 1960s: discontented, unhappy, and critical of everything and everybody.

Tester money (literally, sixpence)
Phrygian Turk barbarous foreigner
operations plots
welkin sky, heavens
eke also
dove will prove wife will try (to seduce)
yellowness jealousy
revolt plot, rebellion (against Falstaff)
old plenty of
King's English see page 163

PISTOL Let vultures gripe thy guts! For gourd and fulham holds,
And high and low beguiles the rich and poor.
Tester I'll have in pouch when thou shalt lack,
Base Phrygian Turk!
NIM I have operations which be humours of revenge.
PISTOL Wilt thou revenge?
NIM By welkin and her star!
PISTOL With wit or steel?
NIM With both the humours, I.
I will discuss the humour of this love to Page.
PISTOL And I to Ford shall eke unfold
How Falstaff, varlet vile,
His dove will prove, his gold will hold,
And his soft couch defile.

NIM My humour shall not cool. I will incense Page to deal with poison. I will possess him with yellowness, for the revolt of mine is dangerous. That is my true humour.

PISTOL Thou art the Mars of malcontents. I second thee. Troop on.

Exeunt

ACT I SCENE 4
Doctor Caius' house

Enter MISTRESS QUICKLY and SIMPLE

MISTRESS QUICKLY What, John Rugby!

[*Enter* RUGBY]

I pray thee, go to the casement and see if you can see my master, Master Doctor Caius, coming. If he do, i'faith, and find anybody in the house, here will be an old abusing of God's patience and the King's English.

RUGBY I'll go watch.

Mistress Quickly comments favourably on John Rugby. After questioning Simple, she says she will help in Slender's wooing of Anne. Doctor Caius' unexpected return prompts her to hide Simple in the medicine cupboard.

---

1 First impressions of Mistress Quickly (in pairs)

Like every other character in the play, Mistress Quickly has her own distinctive language and way of speaking. To gain a first impression of her style, take turns to play Mistress Quickly and Simple, and speak lines 7–29 several times. Afterwards, suggest a number of words or phrases that you think describe her character and her typical way of speaking.

2 Check your impression of Slender

Simple's description of his master may or may not be true. Perhaps he is doing his best to present a favourable picture of Slender. There's no way of knowing if the physical descriptions are accurate (beard, face, walk). Such matters depend on how any production chooses to present Slender. But what about his personality? Is he mild-mannered ('softly-sprighted')?

Think back to what you remember of Slender in Scene 1. Did he strike you as a brave fighter ('as tall a man of his hands')? Is he likely to have 'fought with a warrener' (someone responsible for farming rabbits)?

3 'Into this closet'

Mistress Quickly's order begins what on stage usually becomes an hilarious episode. In Elizabethan times, 'closet' meant a small private room, but in some modern productions Simple is bundled into a large medicine cupboard placed centre-stage. Suggest how you would present 'this closet' to maximise comic effect.

---

posset hot spiced drink
withal with
breed-bate troublemaker (breeder of disputes)
paring-knife knife for cutting leather
Cain-coloured reddish-yellow
between this and his head around here
warrener rabbit-keeper
shent rebuked, blamed
Caius often pronounced as 'Ki-us', but sometimes as 'Keese'
toys trivialities

MISTRESS QUICKLY Go; and we'll have a posset for't soon at night, in faith, at the latter end of a sea-coal fire.

[*Exit Rugby*]

An honest, willing, kind fellow as ever servant shall come in house withal; and, I warrant you, no tell-tale, nor no breed-bate. His worst fault is that he is given to prayer. He is something peevish that way, but nobody but has his fault. But let that pass. Peter Simple you say your name is?

SIMPLE Ay, for fault of a better.

MISTRESS QUICKLY And Master Slender's your master?

SIMPLE Ay, forsooth.

MISTRESS QUICKLY Does he not wear a great round beard like a glover's paring-knife?

SIMPLE No, forsooth. He hath but a little wee face, with a little yellow beard, a Cain-coloured beard.

MISTRESS QUICKLY A softly-sprighted man, is he not?

SIMPLE Ay, forsooth. But he is as tall a man of his hands as any is between this and his head. He hath fought with a warrener.

MISTRESS QUICKLY How say you? – O, I should remember him. Does he not hold up his head, as it were, and strut in his gait?

SIMPLE Yes, indeed does he.

MISTRESS QUICKLY Well, heaven send Anne Page no worse fortune! Tell Master Parson Evans I will do what I can for your master. Anne is a good girl, and I wish –

RUGBY [*Within*] Out, alas! Here comes my master.

MISTRESS QUICKLY We shall all be shent. Run in here, good young man; go into this closet. He will not stay long.

[*He steps into the closet*]

What, John Rugby! John! What, John, I say!

[*Enter* RUGBY]

[*Speaking loudly*] Go, John, go enquire for my master. I doubt he be not well, that he comes not home.

[*Exit Rugby*]

[*Sings*] And down, down, adown-a, etc.

[*Enter* DOCTOR CAIUS]

CAIUS Vat is you sing? I do not like dese toys. Pray you go and vetch me in my closet *une boite en vert* – a box, a green-a box. Do intend vat I speak? A green-a box.

At first, Mistress Quickly manages to prevent Doctor Caius from finding Simple in the closet, but finally Caius discovers him. Greatly agitated, Caius calls for his sword. Mistress Quickly begins to explain.

Simple takes shelter behind Mistress Quickly to hide from the rage of Doctor Caius. At what moment opposite do you think this picture was taken?

1 Doctor Caius provides two clues?

The French that Shakespeare gives to Doctor Caius is sometimes used to suggest that the season is summer (‘*Ma foi, il fait fort chaud*’ = by my faith it is very hot), and that Windsor Castle is preparing for the Garter ceremony (‘*Je m'en vais voir à le* court *la grande affaire*’ = I'm going to see a great ceremony at court). You can find more about these topics on pages 104, 148 and 158.

horn-mad mad as a rampant bull
***Oui, mette-le au mon* pocket** Yes, put it in my pocket.
Dépêche quickly
jack knave
trot faith (troth)
Que ai-je oublié? What have I forgotten?
simples medicinal herbs (and an opportunity for comic business as Mistress Quickly knows Simple is in the closet!)
diable devil
Larron! thief
phlegmatic angry (she means ‘choleric’)

MISTRESS QUICKLY Ay, forsooth. I'll fetch it you. [*Aside*] I am glad he went not in himself. If he had found the young man, he would have been horn-mad.

[*She goes into the closet*]

CAIUS *Fe, fe, fe, fe! Ma foi, il fait fort chaud. Je m'en vais voir à le* court *la grande affaire.*

[*Returning, she shows him the box*]

MISTRESS QUICKLY Is it this, sir?
CAIUS *Oui, mette-le au mon* pocket. *Dépêche*, quickly. Vere is dat knave Rugby?
MISTRESS QUICKLY What, John Rugby! John!

[*Enter* RUGBY]

RUGBY Here, sir.
CAIUS You are John Rugby, and you are jack Rugby. Come, take-a your rapier, and come after my heel to the court.
RUGBY 'Tis ready, sir, here in the porch.
CAIUS By my trot, I tarry too long. 'Od's me! *Que ai-je oublié?* Dere is some simples in my closet, dat I vill not for the varld I shall leave behind.

[*He goes into the closet*]

MISTRESS QUICKLY Ay me, he'll find the young man there, and be mad.
CAIUS [*Within*] O, *diable, diable*! Vat is in my closet? Villainy! *Larron*!

[*He pulls Simple out of the closet*]

Rugby, my rapier!
MISTRESS QUICKLY Good master, be content.
CAIUS Wherefore shall I be content-a?
MISTRESS QUICKLY The young man is an honest man.
CAIUS What shall de honest man do in my closet? Dere is no honest man dat shall come in my closet.
MISTRESS QUICKLY I beseech you, be not so phlegmatic. Hear the truth of it. He came of an errand to me from Parson Hugh.
CAIUS Vell?
SIMPLE Ay, forsooth, to desire her to –
MISTRESS QUICKLY Peace, I pray you.

Simple tells of his errand. Mistress Quickly promises she will help Slender woo Anne. Caius challenges Sir Hugh to a duel, intending to marry Anne himself. Mistress Quickly assures him of Anne's love.

1 **Schemer? Birdbrain?** (in small groups)

Mistress Quickly wants to keep in with everybody. She tells Simple that she will recommend Slender to Anne Page (lines 79–80). Shortly after she tells Doctor Caius that Anne loves him (line 101). When you turn the page you will discover that she also swears that Anne loves Fenton (line 122).

Many critics claim that Mistress Quickly is a butterfly brain, jumping from one point to another, unable to follow a train of thought. But is she as scatterbrained as all that? Take turns to speak everything she says between lines 77–89, then talk together about your impression of her. Is she much more clever than she is usually given credit for?

2 **Sexual meanings?** (in pairs)

Elizabethan audiences saw sexual implications in expressions that may not seem to have such overtones today. Have a guess at the sexual humour in lines 84, 94–5, and 99. If you were directing the play, how might you bring out more clearly the sexual possibilities of the lines?

3 **Doctor Caius: what's he like?** (in small groups)

Doctor Caius is often played as a comic Frenchman: he may murder the English language but for all his threats he intends no real harm to anyone. But some critics claim he represents how much the Elizabethans detested the French, and he is occasionally portrayed as genuinely irritable and malevolent, thoroughly dislikeable. What is your view? Experiment with different ways of speaking Caius' lines opposite (comic, genuinely irate and contemptuous, and so on).

---

ne'er put my finger in the fire won't interfere
baillez fetch
Tarry wait
melancholy angry (she means 'choleric')
jack'nape knave, monkey
gar God
meddle or make interfere
stones testicles
Jarteer Garter
measure our weapon umpire the duel (but 'weapon' has sexual implications)

CAIUS Peace-a your tongue. [*To Simple*] Speak-a your tale.

SIMPLE To desire this honest gentlewoman, your maid, to speak a good word to Mistress Anne Page for my master in the way of marriage.

MISTRESS QUICKLY This is all indeed, la! But I'll ne'er put my finger in the fire, and need not.

CAIUS Sir Hugh send-a you? Rugby, *baillez* me some paper. [*To Simple*] Tarry you a little-a while.

[*Rugby brings paper from the closet. Caius writes*]

MISTRESS QUICKLY [*Aside to Simple*] I am glad he is so quiet. If he had been throughly moved, you should have heard him so loud and so melancholy. But notwithstanding, man, I'll do your master what good I can. And the very yea and the no is, the French doctor, my master – I may call him my master, look you, for I keep his house, and I wash, wring, brew, bake, scour, dress meat and drink, make the beds, and do all myself –

SIMPLE 'Tis a great charge to come under one body's hand.

MISTRESS QUICKLY Are you advised o'that? You shall find it a great charge; and to be up early and down late. But notwithstanding – to tell you in your ear; I would have no words of it – my master himself is in love with Mistress Anne Page. But notwithstanding that, I know Anne's mind. That's neither here nor there.

CAIUS [*Giving a letter to Simple*] You, jack'nape, give-a this letter to Sir Hugh. By gar, it is a shallenge. I will cut his troat in de Park, and I will teach a scurvy jackanape priest to meddle or make. You may be gone. It is not good you tarry here.

[*Exit Simple*]

By gar, I will cut all his two stones. By gar, he shall not have a stone to throw at his dog.

MISTRESS QUICKLY Alas, he speaks but for his friend.

CAIUS It is no matter-a ver dat. Do not you tell-a me dat I shall have Anne Page for myself? By gar, I vill kill de jack priest; and I have appointed mine host of de Jarteer to measure our weapon. By gar, I will myself have Anne Page.

MISTRESS QUICKLY Sir, the maid loves you, and all shall be well. We must give folks leave to prate. What the good-year!

CAIUS Rugby, come to the court with me. [*To Mistress Quickly*] By gar, if I have not Anne Page, I shall turn your head out of my door. – Follow my heels, Rugby.

MISTRESS QUICKLY You shall have An – [*Exeunt Caius and Rugby*]

Mistress Quickly reveals her true opinion of Caius. She tells Fenton that Anne loves him. He pays her money to speak to Anne on his behalf. Alone, she says Anne does not love him.

---

1 Insulting Doctor Caius (in pairs)

Calling after the departing Doctor Caius, Mistress Quickly seems to assure him that Anne Page is his: 'You shall have An – '. But as soon as he is out of earshot she completes her sentence to say what she really thinks of her master: ' – fool's head of your own'. Do you think she should call those words after him, speak them to the audience, or …?

2 Social status

Fenton is the third suitor who hopes to marry Anne Page. He is described in the List of characters as 'a young gentleman'. Identify the different ways in which Mistress Quickly acknowledges his high social status (the first example is 'good worship' in line 114).

3 Does she speak the truth? (in small groups)

a Mistress Quickly makes a good deal of the conversation she had with Anne about the wart above Fenton's eye. Is she speaking truthfully?

b She also claims that she knows Anne's mind. From your acquaintance with her in this scene, do you think that is true?

c Talk together about how far you trust anything that Mistress Quickly says. There is a stage convention that in soliloquy (alone on stage) characters tell the truth. Talk together about whether you think Shakespeare is following or subverting that convention in Mistress Quickly's two soliloquies opposite. For example, do you think her claim that Anne does not love Fenton is true?

---

trow wonder
suit wooing (of Anne)
His hands God's hands
on a book on the Bible
Nan Anne
detest protest
allicholy melancholy
musing thinking
thy voice your support
confidence conversation
Out upon't! Curse it!

– fool's head of your own. No, I know Anne's mind for that. Never a woman in Windsor knows more of Anne's mind than I do, nor can do more than I do with her, I thank heaven.

FENTON [*Within*] Who's within there, ho?

MISTRESS QUICKLY Who's there, I trow? Come near the house, I pray you.

[*Enter* FENTON]

FENTON How now, good woman, how dost thou?

MISTRESS QUICKLY The better that it pleases your good worship to ask.

FENTON What news? How does pretty Mistress Anne?

MISTRESS QUICKLY In truth, sir, and she is pretty, and honest, and gentle, and one that is your friend – I can tell you that by the way, I praise heaven for it.

FENTON Shall I do any good, think'st thou? Shall I not lose my suit?

MISTRESS QUICKLY Troth, sir, all is in His hands above. But notwithstanding, Master Fenton, I'll be sworn on a book she loves you. Have not your worship a wart above your eye?

FENTON Yes, marry, have I. What of that?

MISTRESS QUICKLY Well, thereby hangs a tale. Good faith, it is such another Nan! But, I detest, an honest maid as ever broke bread. We had an hour's talk of that wart. I shall never laugh but in that maid's company. But, indeed, she is given too much to allicholy and musing. But for you – well – go to –

FENTON Well, I shall see her today. Hold, there's money for thee: let me have thy voice in my behalf. If thou seest her before me, commend me –

MISTRESS QUICKLY Will I? I'faith, that we will. And I will tell your worship more of the wart the next time we have confidence, and of other wooers.

FENTON Well, farewell; I am in great haste now.

[*Exit*]

MISTRESS QUICKLY Farewell to your worship. Truly an honest gentleman. But Anne loves him not, for I know Anne's mind as well as another does. – Out upon't! What have I forgot!

[*Exit*]

Looking back at Act 1

Activities for groups or individuals

1 Trouble ahead!

Act 1 sets a number of plots in motion:

- Falstaff, hoping to get his hands on their money, sends letters to Mistress Ford and Mistress Page telling each he loves her.
- Pistol and Nim plan to tell the husbands about Falstaff's love letters.
- Doctor Caius challenges Evans to a duel.
- Three suitors each hope to marry Anne Page: Slender, Caius and Fenton.

Turn to the List of characters on page 1 and rewrite it as a diagram to show these plots. Add illustrations, quotations and comments.

2 Staging Windsor

Some productions open by portraying the bustling life of Windsor, filling the stage with lively action. Read the following account of an English country town written in 1626 and use it, together with your experience of Act 1, to work out how you would present an audience with their first view of Windsor life before Shallow speaks the play's first words.

> 'Six of the clock. It is now the first hour, the sweet time of the morning, and the sun at every window calls the sleepers from their beds. The marigold begins to open her leaves, and the dew on the ground doth sweeten the air. The falconers now meet with many a fair flight, and the hare and the hounds have made the huntsman good sport. The shops in the city begin to shew their wares, and the market people have taken their places. The scholars now have their forms, and whosoever cannot say his lesson must presently look for absolution. The forester is now drawing home to his lodge, and if his deer be gone, he may draw after cold scent. Now begins the curst mistress to put her girls to their tasks, and a lazy hilding (good-for-nothing) will do hurt among good workers. Now the mower falls to whetting of his scythe, and the beaters of hemp give a 'Ho!' to every blow. The ale-knight is at his cup ere he can well see his drink, and the beggar is as nimble-tongued as if he had been at it all day. The fishermen are now at the crayer (boat) for their oysters, and they will never tire crying (= shouting for buyers), while they have one in their basket.'

From left to right: Falstaff, Pistol, Slender, Bardolph. Slender has been robbed by Falstaff's followers, but he gets only threats and disdain from them. Find the moment in Scene 1 when the picture was taken, then say how far this depiction of Falstaff matches your own view of him.

3 Mangling English

One of the major themes of the play is the abuse of the English language (see page 163). Act 1 introduces a number of characters who do just that, using English in their own distinctive style. For example, Nim can hardly utter a sentence without using the word 'humour'. He seems utterly obsessed by it. Give one or two examples of how each of the following characters use English in their own idiosyncratic way: Sir Hugh Evans, Shallow, Mistress Quickly, the Host of the Garter, Pistol, Doctor Caius.

4 Peter Simple's story

Step into role as Peter Simple and tell all you know about what has happened in Windsor so far. You may be very puzzled by events!

Mistress Page is surprised to receive a love letter. She reads it aloud and finds it is Falstaff's declaration of love for her. She condemns Falstaff's character, expresses astonishment, and thinks of revenge.

---

1 Act it out! (in small groups)

Lines 1–25 make great theatre. They tell much about Mistress Page, about Falstaff, and about the Elizabethans. Talk together about the following points, then prepare a presentation of the lines, either by one person or with the whole group sharing the language.

a Which lines might she speak directly to the audience, as if inviting their response?

b Where might she most effectively pause to increase comic effect? What gestures and facial expressions might she use?

c As she reads the letter, might she imitate Falstaff's voice and style of speaking?

d Mistress Page seems far from the stereotype of the submissive Elizabethan woman. She declares she will propose ('exhibit') a bill in parliament to suppress men (lines 23–4), and she is determined to be revenged on Falstaff for his impudence. How can your performance best express her spirited independence?

e Falstaff's letter pompously opens by imitating the style of the Italian poet Petrarch (1304–1374) in its use of personifications: Love might let Reason preach like an austere spiritual guide ('precisian'), but he won't necessarily listen to Reason as a friendly adviser ('counsellor'). After that formal opening the letter becomes a series of rhythmically repetitive exclamations (by no means flattering to Mistress Page), and a simple rhyme. Which sentences are most likely to make Mistress Page grimace?

---

the holiday time of my beauty my youth
there's sympathy how alike we are!
sack Spanish white wine
Herod of Jewry boastful villain of medieval plays
an unweighed unconsidered, ill-judged
Flemish drunkard Elizabethans stereotyped Dutchmen as pot-bellied drunks
conversation speech and behaviour
assay test, attempt to seduce

Act 2 Scene 1
Windsor: a street

Enter MISTRESS PAGE, with a letter

MISTRESS PAGE What, have I 'scaped love-letters in the holiday time of my beauty, and am I now a subject for them? Let me see.

[*She reads*]

'Ask me no reason why I love you, for though Love use Reason for his precisian, he admits him not for his counsellor. You are not young, no more am I. Go to, then, there's sympathy. You are merry, so am I. Ha, ha, then, there's more sympathy. You love sack, and so do I. Would you desire better sympathy? Let it suffice thee, Mistress Page – at the least if the love of soldier can suffice – that I love thee. I will not say, pity me – 'tis not a soldier-like phrase – but I say, love me. By me,

Thine own true knight,
By day or night,
Or any kind of light,
With all his might,
For thee to fight,
John Falstaff.'

What a Herod of Jewry is this! O, wicked, wicked world! One that is well-nigh worn to pieces with age to show himself a young gallant! What an unweighed behaviour hath this Flemish drunkard picked – with the devil's name – out of my conversation, that he dares in this manner assay me? Why, he hath not been thrice in my company. What should I say to him? I was then frugal of my mirth. Heaven forgive me! Why, I'll exhibit a bill in the parliament for the putting down of men. How shall I be revenged on him? For revenged I will be, as sure as his guts are made of puddings. [*She puts away the letter*]

[*Enter* MISTRESS FORD]

MISTRESS FORD Mistress Page! Trust me, I was going to your house.

MISTRESS PAGE And, trust me, I was coming to you. You look very ill.

MISTRESS FORD Nay, I'll ne'er believe that. I have to show to the contrary.

MISTRESS PAGE Faith, but you do, in my mind.

Mistress Ford claims that a sinful act could make her a Lady. She produces the love letter from Falstaff, and thinks of revenge. Mistress Page reveals she has received an identical letter.

---

1 Dialogue (in pairs)

Take parts and experiment with different ways of speaking the conversation in lines 26–43. The Wives are old friends, used to sharing each other's confidences. But as you try out different styles, think about whether they are frank or embarrassed about sexual matters. Just how do they talk about 'one trifling respect' (one small matter), which actually means sleeping with Falstaff, and about 'hack' (line 41) which means going with prostitutes?

2 Soliloquy? (in pairs)

As Mistress Page reads the letter, Alice Ford embarks on what seems like a soliloquy in which she reflects on Falstaff's hypocrisy in appearing so outwardly respectable, but being so false. Her image of how Falstaff's disposition contrasts with his words in the letter is based on the very different musical rhythms of two Elizabethan tunes: 'the Hundredth Psalm' and 'Greensleeves'. His hypocrisy prompts her to think of revenge (just as Mistress Page had done).

Take turns to speak lines 44–53, using your partner as the audience. Try to confide your thoughts to your audience as convincingly as you can.

3 Make them laugh!

Mistress Page has at least two opportunities to make the audience explode with laughter, at lines 55–60 and 60–1. Advise her how to deliver the lines to greatest comic effect. How might she also make the audience laugh at the now obscure meaning of line 64? In Greek mythology, the gods imprisoned giants under Mount Pelion.

---

knighted become a Lady
the article of thy gentry your social status
burn daylight waste time
liking appearance
reproof to all uncomeliness rebuke to improper behaviour
adhere and keep place belong
trow wonder
tuns barrels
put us two seduce us
turtles doves (which are faithful)

MISTRESS FORD Well, I do, then. Yet I say I could show you to the contrary. O Mistress Page, give me some counsel!

MISTRESS PAGE What's the matter, woman?

MISTRESS FORD O woman, if it were not for one trifling respect, I could come to such honour!

MISTRESS PAGE Hang the trifle, woman, take the honour. What is it? Dispense with trifles. What is it?

MISTRESS FORD If I would but go to hell for an eternal moment or so, I could be knighted.

MISTRESS PAGE What? Thou liest! Sir Alice Ford? These knights will hack, and so thou shouldst not alter the article of thy gentry.

MISTRESS FORD We burn daylight. Here, read, read. Perceive how I might be knighted.

[*She produces a letter and gives it to Mistress Page, who reads it*]

I shall think the worse of fat men as long as I have an eye to make difference of men's liking. And yet he would not swear, praised women's modesty, and gave such orderly and well-behaved reproof to all uncomeliness that I would have sworn his disposition would have gone to the truth of his words. But they do no more adhere and keep place together than the Hundredth Psalm to the tune of 'Greensleeves'. What tempest, I trow, threw this whale, with so many tuns of oil in his belly, ashore at Windsor? How shall I be revenged on him? I think the best way were to entertain him with hope till the wicked fire of lust have melted him in his own grease. Did you ever hear the like?

MISTRESS PAGE Letter for letter, but that the name of Page and Ford differs.

[*She holds up her own letter from Falstaff*]

To thy great comfort in this mystery of ill opinions, here's the twin-brother of thy letter. But let thine inherit first, for I protest mine never shall.

[*She gives the two letters to Mistress Ford, who compares them*]

I warrant he hath a thousand of these letters, writ with blank space for different names – sure, more, and these are of the second edition. He will print them, out of doubt; for he cares not what he puts into the press when he would put us two. I had rather be a giantess and lie under Mount Pelion. Well, I will find you twenty lascivious turtles ere one chaste man.

Both Wives are determined to resist Falstaff's advances, but intend to encourage him to disaster. Pistol tells Ford that Falstaff loves his wife, and hints that Ford will become a cuckold.

---

1 What the Elizabethans knew (in small groups)

The play is rich in images familiar to Elizabethans. Imagine you are a group of actors preparing a performance. You are having a discussion about how far your audiences will 'get' the meaning of certain lines. Consider each in turn to find if the group can agree which might be fairly easily understood in your performance.

Lines 71–4: The Wives compare Falstaff's approaches to how ships were attacked by boarding parties. Do you think there are sexual implications in the shipping metaphors of 'above deck' and 'under my hatches'?

Lines 76–7 – 'fine-baited': The image comes from fishing. It implies tempting Falstaff with alluring bait like that on an angler's hook.

Line 77 – 'pawned his horses': For a knight, horses were a symbol of superior status. Sir John Falstaff, having to give up his horses, would be particularly humiliated.

Line 89: 'a curtal dog' was a dog whose tail had been cut off. It was thought of as false, not a proper dog. Pistol implies that Ford's hope is similarly false.

Line 96: The liver was thought to be the seat of the passions.

Lines 97–9: In Greek mythology, Actaeon was turned into a stag and killed by his own hounds (his punishment for watching the goddess Diana bathing naked). The stag's horns were the symbol of cuckoldry: deceived husbands were laughed at as wearing horns. 'Ringwood' was a popular Elizabethan name for a hunting dog.

---

hand handwriting
wrangle with mine own honesty doubt my own virtue
entertain think of
withal with
strain defect, quality
give him a show of comfort in his suit encourage his wooing
sully the chariness of our honesty besmirch our scrupulous virtue
goodman husband
affects loves, lusts after
perpend think about it

MISTRESS FORD Why, this is the very same: the very hand, the very words. What doth he think of us?

MISTRESS PAGE Nay, I know not. It makes me almost ready to wrangle with mine own honesty. I'll entertain myself like one that I am not acquainted withal; for, sure, unless he know some strain in me that I know not myself, he would never have boarded me in this fury.

MISTRESS FORD 'Boarding' call you it? I'll be sure to keep him above deck.

MISTRESS PAGE So will I. If he come under my hatches, I'll never to sea again. Let's be revenged on him. Let's appoint him a meeting, give him a show of comfort in his suit, and lead him on with a fine-baited delay till he hath pawned his horses to mine host of the Garter.

MISTRESS FORD Nay, I will consent to act any villainy against him that may not sully the chariness of our honesty. O that my husband saw this letter! It would give eternal food to his jealousy.

[Enter FORD with PISTOL, and PAGE with NIM]

MISTRESS PAGE Why, look where he comes, and my goodman too. He's as far from jealousy as I am from giving him cause, and that, I hope, is an unmeasurable distance.

MISTRESS FORD You are the happier woman.

MISTRESS PAGE Let's consult together against this greasy knight. Come hither.

[*They withdraw*]

FORD Well, I hope it be not so.

PISTOL Hope is a curtal dog in some affairs.
Sir John affects thy wife.

FORD Why, sir, my wife is not young.

PISTOL He woos both high and low, both rich and poor,
Both young and old, one with another, Ford.
He loves the gallimaufry. Ford, perpend.

FORD Love my wife?

PISTOL With liver burning hot. Prevent,
Or go thou, like Sir Actaeon he,
With Ringwood at thy heels.
O, odious is the name!

Pistol's warning that Ford will be deceived by his wife worries Ford. But Page refuses to believe a similar warning by Nim. The Wives intend to use Mistress Quickly in their plot against Falstaff.

'Take heed.' Ford is warned by Pistol as Page and Nim look on. How does this picture and the language opposite suggest that Ford is worried about his wife's fidelity?

1 Why 'humour'?

Nim's constant use of 'humour' amuses Page: 'Here's a fellow frights English out of his wits.' 'Humour' today means something that makes you laugh, but the word had a very different meaning for Elizabethans, who believed that personality was determined by four 'humours' (fluids in the human body). These were blood (producing bravery), phlegm (producing calmness), 'yellowe' (producing anger), and black bile (producing melancholy). The popular theory of the four humours was used to explain people's behaviour or moods. The belief was that if the four humours were in balance, the result was a healthy and temperate person.

horn sign of a cuckold (see page 38)
cuckoo-birds birds which take over other birds' nests (as Falstaff intends to take over Ford's 'nest'), 'cuckold' derives from 'cuckoo'
bite upon my necessity strike when needed
avouch confirm
quoth'a says he
Cataian Chinaman (from Cathay), Elizabethan stereotype of villain
crotchets silly ideas
forsooth truly

FORD What name, sir?

PISTOL The horn, I say. Farewell.
Take heed, have open eye, for thieves do foot by night.
Take heed, ere summer comes, or cuckoo-birds do sing.
Away, Sir Corporal Nim!
Believe it, Page; he speaks sense. [*Exit*]

FORD I will be patient. I will find out this.

NIM [*To Page*] And this is true. I like not the humour of lying. He hath wronged me in some humours. I should have borne the humoured letter to her, but I have a sword and it shall bite upon my necessity. He loves your wife. There's the short and the long. My name is Corporal Nim. I speak and I avouch. 'Tis true. My name is Nim, and Falstaff loves your wife. Adieu. I love not the humour of bread and cheese. Adieu. [*Exit*]

PAGE The humour of it, quoth'a! Here's a fellow frights English out of his wits.

FORD I will seek out Falstaff.

PAGE I never heard such a drawling, affecting rogue.

FORD If I do find it – well.

PAGE I will not believe such a Cataian, though the priest o'th'town commended him for a true man.

FORD 'Twas a good sensible fellow – well.

[*Mistress Page and Mistress Ford come forward*]

PAGE How now, Meg?

MISTRESS PAGE Whither go you, George? Hark you.

[*They withdraw and talk*]

MISTRESS FORD How now, sweet Frank, why art thou melancholy?

FORD I melancholy? I am not melancholy. Get you home, go.

MISTRESS FORD Faith, thou hast some crotchets in thy head now. –
Will you go, Mistress Page?

MISTRESS PAGE Have with you. – You'll come to dinner, George?

[*Enter* MISTRESS QUICKLY]

[*Aside to Mistress Ford*] Look who comes yonder. She shall be our messenger to this paltry knight.

MISTRESS FORD Trust me, I thought on her. She'll fit it.

MISTRESS PAGE You are come to see my daughter Anne?

MISTRESS QUICKLY Ay, forsooth; and I pray how does good Mistress Anne?

Page dismisses Nim and Pistol as unreliable rogues. He expresses faith in his wife, but Ford is increasingly anxious about his wife's fidelity. Shallow tells of the forthcoming duel between Evans and Caius.

---

1 Casual sexism? (in pairs)

Although the play gives a strong impression that women are fully equal to men, it also contains hints of the sexism and patriarchy that characterised Elizabethan England. Page, unlike Ford, trusts his wife, but he uses an expression about her and Falstaff that some critics find offensive: 'I would turn her loose to him.' The image is of a cow being turned loose to a bull (it also occurs in *Hamlet* Act 2 Scene 2, line 160).

What would you reply to someone who says 'beneath all his friendly manner, the expression shows Ford is an unthinking male chauvinist pig'?

2 Double meaning

The two husbands use the same expression at lines 149 and 151–2, ' lie on my head'. One man is thinking 'that's my responsibility', the other is thinking 'I'll be wearing the cuckold's horns'. Which man has which thought in mind?

3 Oops! Shakespeare in a hurry?

Shallow's greeting 'Good even and twenty' (line 158) is often used as evidence that Shakespeare wrote *Merry Wives* in haste. Looked at one way, it expresses Shallow's repetitive style ('Good evening and many more!'). But in terms of dramatic construction, it seems an error. The time is actually morning, because at line 128 Mistress Page said 'You'll come to dinner, George?' In Elizabethan England, dinner was the main daily meal, eaten around 11 a.m. You can find more on page 182 about the belief that Shakespeare wrote the play in only two weeks.

---

offer it dare, attempt seduction
yoke pair
out of service not employed
Marry by Saint Mary (an oath)
lie at the Garter lodge at the inn
this voyage toward this seduction
loath unwilling
turn them together let my wife and Falstaff meet in private
pate head
Cavaliero swaggering gentleman (Shallow)

MISTRESS PAGE Go in with us and see. We have an hour's talk with you.

[*Exeunt Mistress Page, Mistress Ford, and Mistress Quickly*]

PAGE How now, Master Ford?

FORD You heard what this knave told me, did you not?

PAGE Yes, and you heard what the other told me?

FORD Do you think there is truth in them?

PAGE Hang 'em, slaves! I do not think the knight would offer it. But these that accuse him in his intent towards our wives are a yoke of his discarded men: very rogues, now they be out of service.

FORD Were they his men?

PAGE Marry, were they.

FORD I like it never the better for that. Does he lie at the Garter?

PAGE I, marry, does he. If he should intend this voyage toward my wife, I would turn her loose to him; and what he gets more of her than sharp words, let it lie on my head.

FORD I do not misdoubt my wife, but I would be loath to turn them together. A man may be too confident. I would have nothing lie on my head. I cannot be thus satisfied.

[*Enter* HOST]

PAGE Look where my ranting host of the Garter comes. There is either liquor in his pate or money in his purse when he looks so merrily. How now, mine host?

HOST How now, bully rook? Thou'rt a gentleman. – Cavaliero justice, I say!

[*Enter* SHALLOW]

SHALLOW I follow, mine host, I follow. Good even and twenty, good Master Page. Master Page, will you go with us? We have sport in hand.

HOST Tell him, cavaliero justice; tell him, bully rook.

SHALLOW Sir, there is a fray to be fought between Sir Hugh the Welsh priest and Caius the French doctor.

FORD Good mine host o'th'Garter, a word with you.

HOST What sayst thou, my bully rook?

[*They withdraw and talk*]

Shallow tells how the duel will turn into farce. The Host agrees to arrange that Ford, disguised, meets Falstaff. Shallow boasts of his past prowess in sword-fencing. Ford plans to test his wife's fidelity.

1 Trickster, fixer, embellisher (in small groups)

The Host of the Garter plays an important part in the play.

- He has ensured that the duellists' swords are of equal length ('had the measuring of their weapons'), but has arranged that Evans and Doctor Caius turn up to fight their duel in different locations ('contrary places').
- He fixes that Ford, in disguise, can come and go to Falstaff as he wishes ('egress and regress').
- He flatters other characters, inflating their status with grand titles. Falstaff becomes 'my guest cavalier', the characters on stage are 'ameers': emirs or mynheers (Dutch gentlemen).

Talk together about the actor you would choose to play the Host. What characteristics should he be able to skilfully portray?

2 Not like the old days!

Shallow regrets modern styles of sword-fencing, and looks back to the good old days of long-sword fighting. You can find a more extended criticism of fashionable duelling styles spoken by Mercutio in *Romeo and Juliet* Act 2 Scene 4, lines 18–23.

3 Whisper it! (in pairs)

Ford's jealousy is obviously growing. He is becoming more and more obsessed with the thought that his wife may be deceiving him. Obsessives often whisper their thoughts with great intensity. Take turns to whisper Ford's soliloquy, lines 186–91. Decide what advice you would give Ford about how to deliver the soliloquy on stage.

no jester in deadly earnest
suit legal action
pottle of burnt sack half-gallon tankard of mulled wine
In these times … distance it's fashionable for duellists to be far apart
passes, stoccadoes rapier thrusts
wag go
stands so firmly confidently believes
made got up to
labour well bestowed worthwhile work

SHALLOW [*To Page*] Will you go with us to behold it? My merry host hath had the measuring of their weapons, and, I think, hath appointed them contrary places; for, believe me, I hear the parson is no jester. Hark, I will tell you what our sport shall be.

[*They withdraw and talk*]

HOST [*Coming forward with Ford*] Hast thou no suit against my knight, my guest cavalier?

FORD None, I protest. But I'll give you a pottle of burnt sack to give me recourse to him, and tell him my name is Brook – only for a jest.

HOST My hand, bully. Thou shalt have egress and regress – said I well? – and thy name shall be Brook. It is a merry knight. [*Speaks to all*] Will you go, ameers?

SHALLOW Have with you, mine host.

PAGE I have heard the Frenchman hath good skill in his rapier.

SHALLOW Tut, sir, I could have told you more. In these times you stand on distance, your passes, stoccadoes, and I know not what. 'Tis the heart, Master Page; 'tis here, 'tis here. I have seen the time, with my long sword, I would have made you four tall fellows skip like rats.

HOST Here, boys, here, here! Shall we wag?

PAGE Have with you. I had rather hear them scold than fight.

[*Exeunt Host, Shallow, and Page*]

FORD Though Page be a secure fool and stands so firmly on his wife's frailty, yet I cannot put off my opinion so easily. She was in his company at Page's house, and what they made there I know not. Well, I will look further into't, and I have a disguise to sound Falstaff. If I find her honest, I lose not my labour. If she be otherwise, 'tis labour well bestowed.

[*Exit*]

Falstaff indignantly rejects Pistol, telling how much he has done to protect him. He contemptuously dismisses Pistol's claim to honour, and declares how difficult it is to keep his own honour intact.

1 What a contrast! 'I' versus 'you' (in pairs)

Falstaff's two long speeches are based on his comparison of Pistol with himself. Throughout, the pronouns 'I' and 'my' are fiercely set against 'you' or 'thou'. Take turns to speak as Falstaff and heavily emphasise each personal pronoun (how many are there?). Use your experience of speaking in this way to prepare a performance of the lines.

2 A matter of honour?

Falstaff is enraged that Pistol refused, upon his honour as a soldier, to deliver the love letter to Mistress Ford. He splutters with rage as he expresses incredulity: 'You stand upon your honour?' He tells what he has done to keep his honour intact ('keep the terms of my honour precise' = keep my honour unblemished). But Falstaff has already admitted to having profited from the theft of a fan (lines 11–13), and he owns up to cheating, lying and stealing: 'shuffle', 'hedge', 'lurch' (line 19).

As a knight and a soldier, Falstaff would be expected to jealously guard his honour. But look closely at lines 16–19 and decide whether you think he really knows he has no honour.

3 What does Pistol look like?

Falstaff banishes Pistol 'to your manor of Pickt-hatch', an area of London notorious for thieves and prostitutes. There he can use his short-bladed knife in the crowds ('a short knife and a throng') to steal purses by cutting them from belts. Use Falstaff's description of 'rags' and 'cat-a-mountain' (wildcat) looks to design or describe your impression of Pistol.

---

lay my countenance to pawn profit from my protection
grated upon pleaded to
grate prison bars
gemini pair of twins
tall brave
gratis for nothing, freely
unconfinable baseness unlimited villainy
on the left hand aside
fain obliged
ensconce protectively cover
red-lattice tavern (inns sometimes had wooden lattices for windows)

Act 2 Scene 2
The Garter Inn

Enter FALSTAFF and PISTOL

FALSTAFF I will not lend thee a penny.

PISTOL Why then, the world's mine oyster,
Which I with sword will open.

FALSTAFF Not a penny. I have been content, sir, you should lay my countenance to pawn. I have grated upon my good friends for three reprieves for you and your coach-fellow Nim, or else you had looked through the grate, like a gemini of baboons. I am damned in hell for swearing to gentlemen my friends you were good soldiers and tall fellows. And when Mistress Bridget lost the handle of her fan, I took't upon mine honour thou hadst it not.

PISTOL Didst not thou share? Hadst thou not fifteen pence?

FALSTAFF Reason, you rogue, reason. Think'st thou I'll endanger my soul gratis? At a word, hang no more about me; I am no gibbet for you. Go – a short knife and a throng – to your manor of Pickt-hatch, go! You'll not bear a letter for me, you rogue? You stand upon your honour? Why, thou unconfinable baseness, it is as much as I can do to keep the terms of my honour precise. I, I, I myself sometimes, leaving the fear of God on the left hand and hiding mine honour in my necessity, am fain to shuffle, to hedge, and to lurch; and yet you, you rogue, will ensconce your rags, your cat-a-mountain looks, your red-lattice phrases, and your bold beating oaths, under the shelter of your honour! You will not do it! You!

PISTOL I do relent. What would thou more of man?

[*Enter* ROBIN]

ROBIN Sir, here's a woman would speak with you.

FALSTAFF Let her approach.

[*Enter* MISTRESS QUICKLY]

MISTRESS QUICKLY Give your worship good morrow.

FALSTAFF Good morrow, good wife.

Mistress Quickly swears she is a virgin. To Falstaff's increasing frustration, she rambles and digresses, not telling Falstaff what he wants to know: Mistress Ford's reaction to his letter.

---

1 **Act it out** (in pairs)

The dialogue between Falstaff and Mistress Quickly in lines 26–106 makes entertaining theatre. To gain a first impression of how the two characters talk together, take parts and read the whole episode. Afterwards, work on some of the activities below and on page 50.

a Robin and Pistol (Falstaff's 'own people') do not speak throughout the episode. Advise them how they might behave.

b 'come a little nearer this ways'. Mistress Quickly repeats her request for Falstaff to come closer, but how does he respond?

c In your delivery, try to catch Mistress Quickly's style of speech. She rarely gets straight to the point, being easily distracted by a particular thought and embroidering on it, neglecting to tell what her listener really wants to hear. She is rhythmically repetitive as she gets carried away in telling how Alice Ford has been expensively wooed by knights, lords and gentlemen: 'coach after coach, letter after letter, gift after gift'. She uses malapropisms: 'canaries' for 'quandaries', 'alligant' for 'elegant'.

d How much do you think Mistress Quickly is deliberately delaying in order to whet Falstaff's appetite (and receive a larger reward)? Might she be flattering Falstaff at line 61? He may be a 'pensioner', a gentleman of the royal bodyguard, and she implies they have higher status than earls.

e How would you convey Falstaff's mounting frustration as he is denied news of what he really wants to hear?

---

an't if it
maid virgin
vouchsafe grant
wanton immoral person
canaries quandary, excitement
musk perfume
rushling rustling
eye-wink 'come hither' look
angels gold coins
Mercury messenger of the gods in Roman mythology (Falstaff means 'get on with it!')

MISTRESS QUICKLY Not so, an't please your worship.
FALSTAFF Good maid, then.
MISTRESS QUICKLY I'll be sworn,
As my mother was the first hour I was born.
FALSTAFF I do believe the swearer. What with me?
MISTRESS QUICKLY Shall I vouchsafe your worship a word or two?

FALSTAFF Two thousand, fair woman, and I'll vouchsafe thee the hearing.

MISTRESS QUICKLY There is one Mistress Ford, sir – I pray come a little nearer this ways - I myself dwell with Master Doctor Caius –

FALSTAFF Well, on. Mistress Ford, you say –

MISTRESS QUICKLY Your worship says very true. I pray your worship, come a little nearer this ways.

FALSTAFF I warrant thee nobody hears – [*Indicating Pistol and Robin*] mine own people, mine own people.

MISTRESS QUICKLY Are they so? God bless them and make them his servants!

FALSTAFF Well, Mistress Ford – what of her?

MISTRESS QUICKLY Why, sir, she's a good creature. Lord, Lord, your worship's a wanton! Well, heaven forgive you, and all of us, I pray!

FALSTAFF Mistress Ford – come, Mistress Ford –

MISTRESS QUICKLY Marry, this is the short and the long of it: you have brought her into such a canaries as 'tis wonderful. The best courtier of them all, when the court lay at Windsor, could never have brought her to such a canary. Yet there has been knights, and lords, and gentlemen, with their coaches, I warrant you, coach after coach, letter after letter, gift after gift, smelling so sweetly, all musk, and so rushling, I warrant you, in silk and gold, and in such alligant terms, and in such wine and sugar of the best and the fairest, that would have won any woman's heart, and, I warrant you, they could never get an eye-wink of her. I had myself twenty angels given me this morning, but I defy all angels in any such sort, as they say, but in the way of honesty. And, I warrant you, they could never get her so much as sip on a cup with the proudest of them all, and yet there has been earls – nay, which is more, pensioners – but, I warrant you, all is one with her.

FALSTAFF But what says she to me? Be brief, my good she-Mercury.

Mistress Quickly tells that Mistress Ford will welcome Falstaff when Ford is away. Mistress Page is also welcoming, but her husband is rarely away, so Falstaff should send his page as go-between with a password.

Pistol (right) watches intently as Mistress Quickly tells Falstaff that both Wives intend to deceive their husbands. You will find the reason for Pistol's interest when you turn the page.

1 Nudge-nudge, wink-wink (in pairs)

One actor who played Mistress Quickly said: 'lines 103–4 are a perfect example of "nudge-nudge, wink-wink" humour, and that's how they should be delivered'. Talk together about how far you agree with her.

wot know
frampold difficult, disagreeable
fartuous virtuous
good parts looks? qualities? sexual organs?
infection affection (Shakespeare may be playing with the repetitions of 'Page' and 'page' from lines 90–1)
take all, pay all money to spend as she pleases
list pleases
nay-word password

MISTRESS QUICKLY Marry, she hath received your letter, for the which she thanks you a thousand times, and she gives you to notify that her husband will be absence from his house between ten and eleven.

FALSTAFF Ten and eleven.

MISTRESS QUICKLY Ay, forsooth; and then you may come and see the picture, she says, that you wot of. Master Ford, her husband, will be from home. Alas, the sweet woman leads an ill life with him; he's a very jealousy man; she leads a very frampold life with him, good heart.

FALSTAFF Ten and eleven. Woman, commend me to her. I will not fail her.

MISTRESS QUICKLY Why, you say well. But I have another messenger to your worship. Mistress Page hath her hearty commendations to you too; and let me tell you in your ear, she's as fartuous a civil modest wife, and one, I tell you, that will not miss you morning nor evening prayer, as any is in Windsor, whoe'er be the other. And she bade me tell your worship that her husband is seldom from home, but she hopes there will come a time. I never knew a woman so dote upon a man. Surely, I think you have charms, la! Yes, in truth.

FALSTAFF Not I, I assure thee. Setting the attraction of my good parts aside, I have no other charms.

MISTRESS QUICKLY Blessing on your heart for't!

FALSTAFF But I pray thee tell me this: has Ford's wife and Page's wife acquainted each other how they love me?

MISTRESS QUICKLY That were a jest indeed! They have not so little grace, I hope. That were a trick indeed! But Mistress Page would desire you to send her your little page, of all loves. Her husband has a marvellous infection to the little page; and truly, Master Page is an honest man. Never a wife in Windsor leads a better life than she does. Do what she will, say what she will, take all, pay all, go to bed when she list, rise when she list, all is as she will. And, truly, she deserves it; for if there be a kind woman in Windsor, she is one. You must send her your page, no remedy.

FALSTAFF Why, I will.

MISTRESS QUICKLY Nay, but do so, then; and, look you, he may come and go between you both. And in any case have a nay-word, that you may know one another's mind, and the boy never need to understand anything; for 'tis not good that children should know any wickedness. Old folks, you know, have discretion, as they say, and know the world.

Falstaff rewards Mistress Quickly who leaves, followed by Pistol intent on possessing her. Falstaff praises his body, expecting pleasures ahead. Ford, disguised as Brook, talks of his wealth.

---

1 **Pistol: three lines, two puzzles** (in small groups)

Pistol's speech is in characteristic style. He thinks of Mistress Quickly as a 'punk' (prostitute) and 'one of Cupid's carriers' (love's messengers). His elaborate image pictures her as a ship to be stormed and boarded ('fights' were screens used in sea battles to protect a ship's crew), and to become his 'prize' (Elizabethan sea captains could regard the ships they captured as legitimate booty). Shakespeare may have inserted lines 108–10 as a bridge to *King Henry V* (written shortly after *Merry Wives*) in which Pistol and Quickly are husband and wife.

Suggest answers to two dramatic puzzles posed by Pistol's three lines. First, how might he show signs of interest in Mistress Quickly during his long silence from line 23? Second, why doesn't Falstaff remark on Pistol's departure, and how might he acknowledge it in some non-verbal way?

2 **Disguise?** (in small groups)

A convention of Elizabethan theatre was that any disguise was impenetrable. Ford might turn up as Brook looking virtually the same as he appeared previously. In modern productions, Ford's disguise is sometimes deliberately exaggerated, for example, wearing an obviously false large beard. Talk together about the reasons for the disguise you would recommend Ford adopts. Does he need any disguise at all? (The stage direction at line 124 has been added by a modern editor.)

---

whelm overwhelm, shipwreck
look after desire, look lovingly on
grossly done too fat
would fain wishes to
draught of sack goblet of wine
encompassed won
via! Italian term of encouragement to horses or soldiers, like 'Onward!'
charge you cause you expense
plight condition, position
unseasoned intrusion untimely or unexpected visit

FALSTAFF Fare thee well; commend me to them both. There's my purse; I am yet thy debtor. Boy, go along with this woman.

[*Exeunt Mistress Quickly and Robin*]

This news distracts me.

PISTOL This punk is one of Cupid's carriers.
Clap on more sails; pursue; up with your fights;
Give fire; she is my prize, or ocean whelm them all! [*Exit*]

FALSTAFF Sayst thou so, old Jack? Go thy ways, I'll make more of thy old body than I have done. Will they yet look after thee? Wilt thou, after the expense of so much money, be now a gainer? Good body, I thank thee. Let them say 'tis grossly done; so it be fairly done, no matter.

[*Enter* BARDOLPH *with a goblet of sack*]

BARDOLPH Sir John, there's one Master Brook below would fain speak with you, and be acquainted with you, and hath sent your worship a morning's draught of sack.

FALSTAFF Brook is his name?

BARDOLPH Ay, sir.

FALSTAFF Call him in.

[*Exit Bardolph*]

Such brooks are welcome to me, that o'erflows such liquor. Aha! Mistress Ford and Mistress Page, have I encompassed you? Go to, *via*!

[*Enter* BARDOLPH, *with* FORD *disguised as Brook*]

FORD God bless you, sir.

FALSTAFF And you, sir. Would you speak with me?

FORD I make bold to press with so little preparation upon you.

FALSTAFF You're welcome. What's your will? – Give us leave, drawer.

[*Exit Bardolph*]

FORD Sir, I am a gentleman that have spent much. My name is Brook.

FALSTAFF Good Master Brook, I desire more acquaintance of you.

FORD Good Sir John, I sue for yours: not to charge you, for I must let you understand I think myself in better plight for a lender than you are, the which hath something emboldened me to this unseasoned intrusion; for they say, if money go before, all ways do lie open.

FALSTAFF Money is a good soldier, sir, and will on.

Ford, as Brook, tempts Falstaff with the promise of money, then tells of his illicit love for Mistress Ford. He has attempted to woo her in all kinds of ways, but without success.

---

1 Deceiving Falstaff, deceiving Ford (in pairs)

In lines 129–224, Ford 'sets up' Falstaff to attempt to seduce his wife, and Falstaff reveals that his preparations are well underway and that he will meet Mistress Ford that very morning. To gain a first impression of what is going on, take parts and speak all the dialogue. When you have completed your reading, work on some of the activities below and on page 56.

a Match the following summaries with the lines opposite. Suggest briefly how each might be delivered (spoken and enacted).

- Ford tempts Falstaff with money.
- He flatters Falstaff's self-esteem.
- He promises to tell of his imperfections.
- He hints that Falstaff has committed similar indiscretions.
- He tells how he has lovingly watched Mistress Ford, sometimes paying to do so.
- He has spent money on presents and on finding out what she likes.
- He has constantly pursued her.
- He has had no luck at all!
- He quotes a couplet that declares love is always elusive.
- He compares his love to the Elizabethan custom that declares that anything built on another person's land belongs to that person.

b Talk together about whether you think Falstaff should be played as utterly gullible: only too ready to believe what Ford tells him. Might he show any sign of suspicion?

Troth in truth
discover a thing tell you something
register catalogue
reproof rebuke
doting observance loving devotion
engrossed arranged
fee'd … sight of her paid for brief glimpses of her
on the wing of all occasions constantly
meed reward
importuned propositioned
edifice building

FORD Troth, and I have a bag of money here troubles me. [*He sets it down*] If you will help to bear it, Sir John, take half, or all, for easing me of the carriage.

FALSTAFF Sir, I know not how I may deserve to be your porter.

FORD I will tell you, sir, if you will give me the hearing.

FALSTAFF Speak, good Master Brook. I shall be glad to be your servant.

FORD Sir, I hear you are a scholar – I will be brief with you – and you have been a man long known to me, though I had never so good means as desire to make myself acquainted with you. I shall discover a thing to you wherein I must very much lay open mine own imperfection. But, good Sir John, as you have one eye upon my follies as you hear them unfolded, turn another into the register of your own, that I may pass with a reproof the easier, sith you yourself know how easy it is to be such an offender.

FALSTAFF Very well, sir. Proceed.

FORD There is a gentlewoman in this town – her husband's name is Ford.

FALSTAFF Well, sir.

FORD I have long loved her, and, I protest to you, bestowed much on her, followed her with a doting observance, engrossed opportunities to meet her, fee'd every slight occasion that could but niggardly give me sight of her, not only bought many presents to give her, but have given largely to many to know what she would have given. Briefly, I have pursued her as love hath pursued me, which hath been on the wing of all occasions. But whatsoever I have merited, either in my mind or in my means, meed I am sure I have received none, unless experience be a jewel; that I have purchased at an infinite rate, and that hath taught me to say this:

'Love like a shadow flies when substance love pursues,
Pursuing that that flies, and flying what pursues.'

FALSTAFF Have you received no promise of satisfaction at her hands?

FORD Never.

FALSTAFF Have you importuned her to such a purpose?

FORD Never.

FALSTAFF Of what quality was your love, then?

FORD Like a fair house built on another man's ground, so that I have lost my edifice by mistaking the place where I erected it.

FALSTAFF To what purpose have you unfolded this to me?

Ford, as Brook, praises Falstaff's qualities and pays him to seduce Mistress Ford. Brook can then blackmail her into yielding to him. Falstaff reveals that he is to meet Mistress Ford this morning.

---

1 The perfect courtier? (in small groups)

Ford's praise of Falstaff echoes *The Courtier* by the Italian Count Baldessare Castiglione, published in English in 1561. This handbook of courtesy defined the Renaissance ideal of the 'complete man'. Talk together about the seven qualities Ford names in lines 177–80. Express each in your own words and say how far you think Falstaff matches up to each.

2 'Understand my drift' (in small groups)

It's little wonder that Falstaff is puzzled by Master Brook's proposal that he woo Mistress Ford. Here's a man who declares he is madly in love with a woman, and yet is forcing money on Falstaff to seduce her! Falstaff wonders how can it suit Brook's overwhelming love ('apply well to the vehemency of your affection') to do such a thing. It's preposterous!

'Understand my drift' (know my purpose) replies Brook (Ford). He explains that Mistress Ford is the very model of virtue. Honour shines out of her like the sun. But if Brook can face her with proof she has been seduced by Falstaff, he can overcome all her defences and possess her himself. Talk together about whether you think that Ford should deliver lines 190–7 convincingly and rationally, or in an obviously exaggerated way.

3 'O good sir!'

Line 201 can be supremely comic as Ford struggles to control his emotions, saying quite the opposite of what he really feels and thinks. How would you speak the line as Ford?

---

enlargeth her mirth plays around
shrewd construction made malicious rumours spread
of great admittance welcomed by noble families
authentic respected
generally allowed approved by all
lay an amiable siege to the honesty of attempt to seduce
instance and argument actual examples
ward of her purity protection of her virtue
speed succeed

FORD When I have told you that, I have told you all. Some say that though she appear honest to me, yet in other places she enlargeth her mirth so far that there is shrewd construction made of her. Now, Sir John, here is the heart of my purpose: you are a gentleman of excellent breeding, admirable discourse, of great admittance, authentic in your place and person, generally allowed for your many warlike, courtlike, and learned preparations.

FALSTAFF O, sir!

FORD Believe it, for you know it. [*Pointing to the bag*] There is money. Spend it, spend it; spend more; spend all I have. Only give me so much of your time in exchange of it as to lay an amiable siege to the honesty of this Ford's wife. Use your art of wooing, win her to consent to you. If any man may, you may as soon as any.

FALSTAFF Would it apply well to the vehemency of your affection that I should win what you would enjoy? Methinks you prescribe to yourself very preposterously.

FORD O, understand my drift. She dwells so securely on the excellency of her honour that the folly of my soul dares not present itself. She is too bright to be looked against. Now, could I come to her with any detection in my hand, my desires had instance and argument to commend themselves. I could drive her then from the ward of her purity, her reputation, her marriage vow, and a thousand other her defences, which now are too too strongly embattled against me. What say you to't, Sir John?

FALSTAFF Master Brook, I will first make bold with your money; [*He takes the bag*] next, give me your hand; and last, as I am a gentleman, you shall, if you will, enjoy Ford's wife.

FORD O good sir!

FALSTAFF I say you shall.

FORD Want no money, Sir John; you shall want none.

FALSTAFF Want no Mistress Ford, Master Brook; you shall want none. I shall be with her, I may tell you, by her own appointment. Even as you came in to me, her assistant or go-between parted from me. I say I shall be with her between ten and eleven, for at that time the jealous rascally knave her husband will be forth. Come you to me at night; you shall know how I speed.

FORD I am blest in your acquaintance. Do you know Ford, sir?

Falstaff, unaware that Brook is Ford, tells how he will have Ford's money and mocks him as a cuckold. Alone on stage, Ford explodes at the thought of becoming a cuckold. He plans to prevent it.

---

1 'Cuckold': the worst insult

Falstaff reveals his real intention in planning to seduce Mistress Ford: he wants to get his hands on Ford's money. His plans and mockery wound Ford deeply, but the insult that really hurts is 'cuckold': a deceived husband. Ford feels that Falstaff's actions will cause him to be called all kinds of detestable names: 'stand under the adoption of abominable terms', like those of various devils. But even worse is 'cuckold' ('wittol' had the same meaning).

To help you prepare a performance of Ford's soliloquy in lines 225–45, work on the following activities.

a The soliloquy is mainly a long series of short explosive thoughts, which reveal Ford's disturbed feelings. To experience the intensity and movement of his emotions, speak the lines, turning abruptly in your seat at each new thought or sentence (if you have space, try this activity walking around the room, changing direction at each thought or sentence).

b Some sentences are lists which pile up item on item. Find each such sentence and speak it aloud. Give each 'item' a different vocal emphasis, and accompany each with a gesture or action (for example, you might 'tick off' the items on your fingers as you speak). The first such list is, 'My wife hath sent to him, the hour is fixed, the match is made.'

c Lines 236–7 express Elizabethan prejudices (Dutchmen 'Fleming[s]' as thieves, Welshmen as lovers of cheese, Irishmen as drunks). Do you think, in the context of the play, such stereotyping is offensive?

---

wittolly cuckoldly (deceived)
coffer money chest
my harvest-home the fruits of my labours
mechanical vulgar, low status
salt-butter cheapskate (imported salt-butter was cheap)
aggravate his style add 'cuckold' to his titles
epicurean sensual, sexy
improvident groundless, rash
aquavitae spirits, e.g. brandy
ambling gelding gentle horse
effect perform, accomplish

FALSTAFF Hang him, poor cuckoldy knave! I know him not. Yet I wrong him to call him poor. They say the jealous wittolly knave hath masses of money, for the which his wife seems to me well-favoured. I will use her as the key of the cuckoldy rogue's coffer, and there's my harvest-home.

FORD I would you knew Ford, sir, that you might avoid him if you saw him.

FALSTAFF Hang him, mechanical salt-butter rogue! I will stare him out of his wits. I will awe him with my cudgel; it shall hang like a meteor o'er the cuckold's horns. Master Brook, thou shalt know I will predominate over the peasant, and thou shalt lie with his wife. Come to me soon at night. Ford's a knave, and I will aggravate his style: thou, Master Brook, shalt know him for knave and cuckold. Come to me soon at night.

[*Exit*]

FORD What a damned epicurean rascal is this! My heart is ready to crack with impatience. Who says this is improvident jealousy? My wife hath sent to him, the hour is fixed, the match is made. Would any man have thought this? See the hell of having a false woman! My bed shall be abused, my coffers ransacked, my reputation gnawn at; and I shall not only receive this villainous wrong, but stand under the adoption of abominable terms, and by him that does me this wrong. Terms! Names! Amaimon sounds well; Lucifer, well; Barbason, well; yet they are devils' additions, the names of fiends: but Cuckold! Wittol! – Cuckold? the devil himself hath not such a name. Page is an ass, a secure ass. He will trust his wife, he will not be jealous. I will rather trust a Fleming with my butter, Parson Hugh the Welshman with my cheese, an Irishman with my aquavitae bottle, or a thief to walk my ambling gelding, than my wife with herself. Then she plots, then she ruminates, then she devises. And what they think in their hearts they may effect, they will break their hearts but they will effect. God be praised for my jealousy! Eleven o'clock the hour: I will prevent this, detect my wife, be revenged on Falstaff, and laugh at Page. I will about it. Better three hours too soon than a minute too late. Fie, fie, fie! Cuckold, cuckold, cuckold!

[*Exit*]

Doctor Caius waits in vain for Sir Hugh Evans to appear and fight. The Host of the Garter mocks Caius unmercifully, relying on the Frenchman's ignorance of English.

---

1 Mocking a foreigner (in small groups)

In Scene 1 of Act 2 (line 168), Shallow reported that the Host of the Garter had played a trick on Caius and Evans, sending them to different places to fight their duel. Now Scene 3 presents Doctor Caius frustrated by Evans' non-arrival, and believing that the Welshman's cowardice keeps him away.

The Host of the Garter's style seems to be one of hearty friendship. But Scene 3 reveals that he takes advantage of Doctor Caius' poor grasp of the English language to ridicule him.

Lines 19-20: He piles up a list of sword-fencing tactics, grossly exaggerating all the techniques Caius might use.

Lines 21–3: He calls Caius 'Ethiopian' (Elizabethans used the term as an insult for any dark-skinned person), 'Francisco' (Frenchman), 'Aesculapius' (Roman god of medicine), and 'Galen' (famous Greek physician). The last two again might seem to flatter Caius, but are really 'over-the-top' ridicule.

Line 23: He implies Caius is a coward: 'heart of elder' might sound like 'heart of oak' (brave), but elder is a weak, soft-centred plant.

Lines 23 and 26: The Host uses the fact that Elizabethan doctors used patients' urine for diagnosis to again insult Caius: 'stale' is horses' urine, and 'Castalion king-urinal' suggests Caius is like Castiglione's courtier (see page 56), but a courtier of urinals!

Work together on all the Host says opposite to find an effective way of how he might deliver the lines on stage. Caius should be unaware that he is being mocked, but the audience should be in on the joke.

Vat is the clock what's the time
Pible Bible
herring 'dead as a herring' was a common Elizabethan expression
foin, traverse, pass, punto, stock, reverse different kinds of fencing thrusts
distance (between two swordsmen)
montant upward rapier thrust
Hector brave Trojan warrior (Is the Host's 'Greece' a mistake or another insult?)

ACT 2 SCENE 3
Windsor: a field

Enter CAIUS and RUGBY, with rapiers

CAIUS Jack Rugby!

RUGBY Sir?

CAIUS Vat is the clock, jack?

RUGBY 'Tis past the hour, sir, that Sir Hugh promised to meet.

CAIUS By gar, he has save his soul dat he is no come. He has pray his Pible well dat he is no come. By gar, jack Rugby, he is dead already if he be come.

RUGBY He is wise, sir. He knew your worship would kill him if he came.

CAIUS By gar, de herring is no dead so as I vill kill him. [*He draws his rapier*] Take your rapier, jack. I vill tell you how I vill kill him.

RUGBY Alas, sir, I cannot fence.

CAIUS Villainy! Take your rapier.

RUGBY Forbear. Here's company.

[*Caius sheathes his rapier*]

[*Enter* HOST, SHALLOW, SLENDER, *and* PAGE]

HOST God bless thee, bully doctor!

SHALLOW God save you, Master Doctor Caius!

PAGE Now, good Master Doctor!

SLENDER Give you good morrow, sir.

CAIUS Vat be all you, one, two, tree, four, come for?

HOST To see thee fight, to see thee foin, to see thee traverse; to see thee here, to see thee there; to see thy pass, thy punto, thy stock, thy reverse, thy distance, thy montant. Is he dead, my Ethiopian? Is he dead, my Francisco? Ha, bully? What says my Aesculapius, my Galen, my heart of elder, ha? Is he dead, bully stale? Is he dead?

CAIUS By gar, he is de coward jack priest of de vorld. He is not show his face.

HOST Thou art a Castalion king-urinal! Hector of Greece, my boy!

CAIUS I pray you bear witness that me have stay six or seven, two, tree hours for him, and he is no come.

Shallow argues that Caius should not fight because he is a doctor. He recalls his own youthful bravery. The Host again mocks Caius, and plans to take him to Frogmore where Evans waits.

---

1 'A great fighter' (in pairs)

Shallow's acknowledgement of Page's compliment (line 32), and his claim that his 'finger itches' to join in a fight have echoes of his claims in *King Henry IV Part 2*, where he presented himself as a courageous madcap in his youth. But in that play Falstaff provides a much more realistic appraisal of the youthful Shallow:

> 'Lord, Lord, how subject we old men are to this vice of lying! This same starved justice hath done nothing but prate to me of the wildness of his youth and the feats he hath done about Turnbull Street, and every third word a lie, duer paid to the hearer than the Turk's tribute. I do remember him at Clement's Inn, like a man made after a supper of a cheese-paring. When a was naked, he was, for all the world, like a forked radish, with a head fantastically carved upon it with a knife … And now is this Vice's dagger become a squire, and talks as familiarly of John a'Gaunt as if he had been sworn brother to him, and I'll be sworn a ne'er saw him but once in the tilt-yard, and then burst his head for crowding among the marshall's men.'
> (*King Henry IV Part 2* Act 3 Scene 2, lines 246–62)

Use Falstaff's description and what you have experienced of Shallow in *Merry Wives* to suggest what you think of Shallow's claim to bravery.

2 More mockery of Doctor Caius

The Host once again ridicules Caius with 'clapper-claw', lying about its meaning (thrash). But what might 'Mockwater' mean? It certainly does not mean 'valour' as the Host claims when Caius questions him. It may be that once again the Host was thinking of how Elizabethan doctors examined the colour and smell of their patients' urine (water).

---

against the hair of contrary to (literally, rub the wrong way)
Bodykins by God's body (an oath)
of the peace a magistrate, justice of the peace
salt savour, strong recollections
sons of women (like all men)
guest justice (Shallow is lodging at the Garter)
jack-dog deceitful animal
wag leave
eke also
Frogmore see map on page 164

SHALLOW He is the wiser man, Master Doctor. He is a curer of souls, and you a curer of bodies. If you should fight, you go against the hair of your professions. Is it not true, Master Page?

PAGE Master Shallow, you have yourself been a great fighter, though now a man of peace.

SHALLOW Bodykins, Master Page, though I now be old and of the peace, if I see a sword out, my finger itches to make one. Though we are justices and doctors and churchmen, Master Page, we have some salt of our youth in us. We are the sons of women, Master Page.

PAGE 'Tis true, Master Shallow.

SHALLOW It will be found so, Master Page. – Master Doctor Caius, I am come to fetch you home. I am sworn of the peace. You have showed yourself a wise physician, and Sir Hugh hath shown himself a wise and patient churchman. You must go with me, Master Doctor.

HOST Pardon, guest justice. – [*To Caius*] A word, Monsieur Mockwater.

CAIUS Mockvater? Vat is dat?

HOST Mockwater, in our English tongue, is valour, bully.

CAIUS By gar, then I have as much mockvater as de Englishman. Scurvy jack-dog priest! By gar, me vill cut his ears.

HOST He will clapper-claw thee tightly, bully.

CAIUS Clapper-de-claw? Vat is dat?

HOST That is, he will make thee amends.

CAIUS By gar, me do look he shall clapper-de-claw me, for, by gar, me vill have it.

HOST And I will provoke him to't, or let him wag.

CAIUS Me tank you for dat.

HOST And moreover, bully – but first, Master guest, and Master Page, and eke Cavaliero Slender, [*Aside*] go you through the town to Frogmore.

PAGE [*Aside to Host*] Sir Hugh is there, is he?

HOST [*Aside to Page*] He is there. See what humour he is in; and I will bring the doctor about by the fields. Will it do well?

SHALLOW [*Aside to Host*] We will do it.

Doctor Caius vows to kill Evans. The Host urges patience and proposes they go to see Anne Page at Frogmore. Caius, grateful, promises he will recommend high-status guests to the Garter tavern.

1 Who is the 'jackanape'? (in small groups)

The 'duel' plot is soon to be resolved as Page, Shallow and Slender leave for Frogmore to meet Sir Hugh Evans, and are followed by the Host and Doctor Caius. But there is a curious puzzle in Caius' rage at Evans having supported the wooing of 'a jackanape' for the hand of Anne Page (line 66). Does he realise that the 'jackanape' is Slender? Is this another sign of Shakespeare's having written the play in haste? Talk together about your own views on why Doctor Caius does not know the identity of his rival wooer.

2 Elizabethan pastimes (in small groups)

The Host's mention that Anne Page is 'at a farmhouse a-feasting' is a reminder of a familiar custom in Elizabethan England. Parties of town dwellers would walk into the country and take a meal and drinks at a farmhouse. Suggest ways in which that custom has survived to the present day.

3 Close to the court

Doctor Caius is delighted by the Host's promise of a meeting with Anne. In return, he promises that he will use his influence to ensure that his top quality patients lodge at the Garter tavern. His list of 'de earl, de knight, de lords, de gentlemen' suggests that Caius is a doctor to the court in Windsor: he has important connections. But Shakespeare may also have invented the list to amuse a royal audience. You can find details on page 186 of the belief that the first performance of the play took place before Queen Elizabeth I and her court.

---

choler anger
'Cried game!' 'How's that!', 'Success!' (a hunting cry?)
adversary advocate (the Host again mocks Caius, saying the opposite of what he means)
jack Rugby Rugby's name is John, but Caius always calls him 'jack' (knave). Is that because of Caius' forgetfulness, poor English, or ill nature?

PAGE, SHALLOW, and SLENDER Adieu, good Master Doctor.

[*Exeunt Page, Shallow, and Slender*]

CAIUS By gar, me vill kill de priest, for he speak for a jackanape to Anne Page.

HOST Let him die. Sheathe thy impatience; throw cold water on thy choler. Go about the fields with me through Frogmore. I will bring thee where Mistress Anne Page is, at a farmhouse a-feasting; and thou shalt woo her. 'Cried game!' Said I well?

CAIUS By gar, me dank you vor dat. By gar, I love you, and I shall procure-a you de good guest: de earl, de knight, de lords, de gentlemen, my patients.

HOST For the which I will be thy adversary toward Anne Page. Said I well?

CAIUS By gar, 'tis good. Vell said.

HOST Let us wag, then.

CAIUS Come at my heels, jack Rugby.

[*Exeunt*]

Looking back at Act 2

Activities for groups or individuals

1 Plot, counter-plot, jealousy

Most of Act 2 is concerned with Falstaff's plan to seduce the Wives for their money. It shows their outraged but amused reaction, and their decision to take revenge. As a result, Ford's jealousy becomes more and more obsessive. Select brief quotations that show these developments as the act progresses, and present them either as a visual display (for example, an illustrated poster), or in a short performance.

2 Bully Bottom?

The Host of the Garter Inn has sometimes been described as like Bottom in *A Midsummer Night's Dream*, expansive and full of self-confidence. Find a copy of *Dream*, read some of Bottom's lines, and give your own judgement on how alike the two characters seem to you.

3 Prepare a prop: the letter

Make a copy of Falstaff's letter (Scene 1, lines 3–16) that could be used in a stage performance. In Shakespeare's day, such a letter might have been attached to a wooden rod around which it was rolled and sealed.

4 Briefing Mistress Quickly

Shakespeare does not show the scene in which Mistress Ford and Mistress Page take Mistress Quickly into their confidence and explain their plan that she be their go-between to fool Falstaff. Step into role as the three women and improvise the missing scene!

5 What's in a name?

Shakespeare sometimes gives characters names that suggests what he or she is like. For example, in *Twelfth Night* Malvolio means 'wishing ill', and in *Merry Wives* 'Nim' meant 'thief' to Elizabethans. From your experience of the play so far, write down two or three words that are suggested by each of the following characters' names: Shallow, Slender, Pistol, Simple, Mistress Quickly.

Mistress Ford and Mistress Page explode with laughter at the thought of their planned revenge on Falstaff. Compare this picture with pages 84, 167, 171, 187. Which comes closest to your own view of the Wives?

Sir Hugh Evans is prepared to fight, but there is no sign of Doctor Caius. Evans feels mixed emotions. He sings, bringing himself close to tears. Simple reports three imminent arrivals.

---

1 'Every way'

Just where has Simple looked for Doctor Caius? You can find a map of Windsor and its surrounds on page 164.

2 Book and rapier (in pairs)

Sir Hugh Evans is a schoolteacher and a priest. But here he is, about to fight a duel! Shakespeare brings out the incongruity by having him carry a book in one hand and a rapier in the other. Many critics have assumed the book is the Bible, but what else might it be? Let your imaginations run and suggest some possible titles (actual or invented) for the book. For example, in one production he carried a copy of *War and Peace*, which emphasised the conflict of his roles.

3 Mixed emotions (in pairs)

Evans' feelings are a mixture of anger ('cholers'), fear and melancholy. He hopes that Caius is deceiving him and will not turn up (line 9), but moments later vows to beat him. He tries to steady himself by singing. Perhaps appropriately, because he is about to fight a duel over love, he sings a version of Christopher Marlowe's *The Passionate Shepherd to His Love*, a famous Elizabethan love lyric which begins 'Come live with me, and be my love, And we will all the pleasures prove.' But he breaks off, near to tears, and inserts a line (19) from Psalm 137, a lament of exile.

Work carefully through all Evans says opposite and suggest his emotions at each moment. Take turns to speak his lines to express his swiftly changing emotions.

Petty-ward Windsor Little Park
Park-ward Windsor Great Park
trempling trembling
urinals Caius' urine specimen bottle, testicles
costard head
'ork work, fight
falls waterfalls
peds beds
posies bunches of flowers
Pabylon Babylon
vagrom fragrant

Act 3 Scene 1
A field near Frogmore

Enter EVANS *with a book in one hand and a drawn rapier in the other, and* SIMPLE *carrying Evans' gown*

EVANS I pray you now, good Master Slender's serving-man, and friend Simple by your name, which way have you looked for Master Caius, that calls himself Doctor of Physic?

SIMPLE Marry, sir, the Petty-ward, the Park-ward, every way; Old Windsor way, and every way but the town way.

EVANS I most fehemently desire you you will also look that way.

SIMPLE I will, sir. [*Going aside*]

EVANS Pless my soul, how full of cholers I am, and trempling of mind! I shall be glad if he have deceived me. How melancholies I am! I will knog his urinals about his knave's costard when I have good opportunities for the 'ork. Pless my soul!

[*Sings*] To shallow rivers, to whose falls
Melodious birds sings madrigals.
There will we make our peds of roses
And a thousand fragrant posies.
To shallow –

Mercy on me! I have a great dispositions to cry.

[*Sings*] Melodious birds sing madrigals –
Whenas I sat in Pabylon –
And a thousand vagrom posies.
To shallow, etc.

SIMPLE Yonder he is coming, this way, Sir Hugh.

EVANS He's welcome.

[*Sings*] To shallow rivers, to whose falls –
Heaven prosper the right! What weapons is he?

SIMPLE No weapons, sir. There comes my master, Master Shallow, and another gentleman, from Frogmore, over the stile, this way.

EVANS Pray you, give me my gown – or else keep it in your arms.

Page and Shallow tease Evans. They tell of Caius' disturbed condition, but Evans expresses contempt for him. A fight seems likely, but Evans and Caius are disarmed.

---

1 Who?

Shallow is probably joking at Simple's expense when he says that Evans' duel keeps 'a good student from his book'. But who might he mean when he says 'Keep a gamester from the dice'. Make your guess who the 'gamester' (gambler) might be.

2 Mocking the middle class? (in pairs)

Shallow and Page are part of the Host's plot to fool Caius and Evans into turning up at different places to fight. Now they gently tease Evans, expressing mock surprise at his appearance. Shallow, seeing what Evans has in each hand, innocently asks if the schoolmaster studies both 'the sword and the word' (the rapier and the Bible). Page adds to Evans' discomfiture by remarking how unsuitably dressed he is for such a cold day ('doublet and hose' = close-fitting jacket and stockings).

Some critics think that the mocking comments of Shallow and Page represent aristocratic attitudes to Evans' and Caius' duel. The Elizabethan nobility thought that duelling was an elite practice. They scorned the idea of middle-class citizens challenging each other in the style of higher-status nobles. Talk together about whether you think it likely that Shakespeare had this aristocratic perspective on duelling in mind as he wrote the whole duel episode.

3 Nearly a fight! (in groups of six or more)

Take parts and work out how to stage the sequence from lines 58–63, in which Evans and Caius square up to each other but are disarmed by Shallow and Page.

---

good office valuable duty
reverend respectable
at most odds … patience battling with conflicting feelings
so wide of his own respect thinking so little of himself
as lief as soon
mess of porridge bowl of thick soup
Hibbocrates Hippocrates, Greek founding father of medicine
Galen famous Greek physician
question talk (rather than fight)
hack chop up (see page 163)

[*Enter* PAGE, SHALLOW, *and* SLENDER]

SHALLOW How now, Master Parson? Good morrow, good Sir Hugh. Keep a gamester from the dice, and a good student from his book, and it is wonderful.

SLENDER Ah, sweet Anne Page!

PAGE God save you, good Sir Hugh!

EVANS God pless you from his mercy sake, all of you!

SHALLOW What, the sword and the word? Do you study them both, Master Parson?

PAGE And youthful still, in your doublet and hose this raw rheumatic day?

EVANS There is reasons and causes for it.

PAGE We are come to you to do a good office, Master Parson.

EVANS Fery well. What is it?

PAGE Yonder is a most reverend gentleman who, belike having received wrong by some person, is at most odds with his own gravity and patience that ever you saw.

SHALLOW I have lived fourscore years and upward. I never heard a man of his place, gravity, and learning so wide of his own respect.

EVANS What is he?

PAGE I think you know him: Master Doctor Caius, the renowned French physician.

EVANS Got's will and his passion of my heart! I had as lief you would tell me of a mess of porridge.

PAGE Why?

EVANS He has no more knowledge in Hibbocrates and Galen – and he is a knave besides, a cowardly knave as you would desires to be acquainted withal.

PAGE [*To Shallow*] I warrant you, he's the man should fight with him.

SLENDER O sweet Anne Page!

SHALLOW It appears so by his weapons. Keep them asunder; here comes Doctor Caius.

[*Enter* CAIUS, HOST, *and* RUGBY. *Evans and Caius offer to fight.*]

PAGE Nay, good Master Parson, keep in your weapon.

SHALLOW So do you, good Master Doctor.

HOST Disarm them, and let them question. Let them keep their limbs whole and hack our English.

[*Shallow and Page take Caius' and Evans' rapiers*]

Evans tries to make peace with Caius. The Host explains: not wishing to lose doctor or priest, he sent them to different locations. Evans and Caius, now friends, vow revenge on the Host.

---

1 Reconcilement – and revenge! (in pairs)

Evans is ready to make peace. Unheard by the others he offers friendship to Caius, urging they should not become laughing stocks. But outwardly Evans keeps up the show of bold anger against the doctor, threatening violence. Take parts as Evans and Caius. Work out how to stage lines 64–76 and 92–9 to show their reconciliation and how they plan to take revenge on the Host.

2 Catch the Host's style! (in small groups)

The Host's typically exuberant speeches in lines 77–8 and 80–9 contain short sentences with similar structures and possess striking rhythm and balance. He balances pairs of words against each other, for example 'Gallia and Gaul' (Wales and France), 'soul-curer and body-curer' (priest and doctor), 'the potions and the motions' (drugs to relieve constipation – and their consequences!), 'the proverbs and the no-verbs' (wise sayings and non-existent words), 'terrestrial', 'celestial' (concerned with earthly matters – medicine, or spiritual matters – religion), 'Your hearts are mighty, your skins are whole' (you are brave and unharmed).

As one person speaks the Host's lines, the others quietly echo any repeated or 'balancing' expressions and accompany them with a 'balancing action' (for example, 'weighing' with your hands).

3 'O sweet Anne Page!'

Slender is caught up in a world of his own. He takes no part in the proceedings, but punctuates the scene with his love-lorn cry 'O sweet Anne Page!'. Suggest how Slender behaves throughout the scene.

Machiavel crafty schemer (Niccolò Machiavelli's book *The Prince*, 1513/1532, advised rulers to practise any deceit to remain in power)
Boys of art men of learning
burnt sack mulled wine
to pawn out of use, as a pledge
sot fool
vlouting-stog laughing stock
scall scabby
cogging companion cheating rogue
noddles head, brains

CAIUS I pray you let-a me speak a word with your ear. Verefore vill you not meet-a me?

EVANS [*Aside to Caius*] Pray you, use your patience. [*Aloud*] In good time.

CAIUS By gar, you are de coward, de jack dog, John ape.

EVANS [*Aside to Caius*] Pray you, let us not be laughing-stocks to other men's humours. I desire you in friendship, and I will one way or other make you amends. [*Aloud*] I will knog your urinal about your knave's cogscomb.

CAIUS *Diable!* Jack Rugby, mine host de Jarteer, have I not stay for him to kill him? Have I not, at de place I did appoint?

EVANS As I am a Christians soul, now look you, this is the place appointed. I'll be judgement by mine host of the Garter.

HOST Peace, I say, Gallia and Gaul, French and Welsh, soul-curer and body-curer.

CAIUS Ay, dat is very good, *excellent.*

HOST Peace, I say. Hear mine host of the Garter. Am I politic? Am I subtle? Am I a Machiavel? Shall I lose my doctor? No; he gives me the potions and the motions. Shall I lose my parson, my priest, my Sir Hugh? No; he gives me the proverbs and the no-verbs. [*To Caius*] Give me thy hand, terrestrial; so. [*To Evans*] Give me thy hand, celestial; so. Boys of art, I have deceived you both. I have directed you to wrong places. Your hearts are mighty, your skins are whole, and let burnt sack be the issue. [*To Page and Shallow*] Come, lay their swords to pawn. [*To Caius and Evans*] Follow me, lads of peace; follow, follow, follow. [*Exit*]

SHALLOW Trust me, a mad host. Follow, gentlemen, follow.

SLENDER O sweet Anne Page!

[*Exeunt Shallow, Slender, and Page*]

CAIUS Ha, do I perceive dat? Have you make-a de sot of us, ha, ha?

EVANS This is well. He has made us his vlouting-stog. I desire you that we may be friends, and let us knog our prains together to be revenge on this same scall, scurvy, cogging companion, the host of the Garter.

CAIUS By gar, with all my heart. He promise to bring me where is Anne Page. By gar, he deceive me too.

EVANS Well, I will smite his noddles. Pray you follow.

[*Exeunt*]

Robin is leading Mistress Page to meet Mistress Ford. Ford's remark reveals that the Wives are very close friends. The news that Robin is Falstaff's page makes a strong impression on Ford.

---

1 'I see you'll be a courtier' (in pairs)

Playwrights sometimes write a line or episode intended especially to please a particular audience. Mistress Page's lines 6–7 is almost certainly such an example. It may make the whole audience laugh, but it had special appeal to Queen Elizabeth I and her courtiers (who are reputed to be the play's first audience, see page 186). But the lines may equally well be a criticism of courtiers, portraying them simply as flatterers.

This is the first time Robin has spoken in the play, but what is your initial impression of him?

2 Sour or straightforward? (in pairs)

Does Ford make his comment about the Wives' close friendship (lines 10–11) sourly, just as a matter of fact or in some other way? Give reasons for your decision.

3 'What the dickens' (in pairs)

Shakespeare is thought to be the first person to use the expression in line 14 which has now become proverbial. What other familiar expressions do you know that come from Shakespeare's plays? You can find a few such examples for *Merry Wives* on page 181.

4 'Sir John Falstaff!' (whole class)

Ford is obsessed with the thought that his wife intends to have sexual relations with Falstaff. So how does he speak line 17? One person compiles a list of suggestions made by the whole class. Which suggestions occur most frequently?

---

keep your way keep ahead
gallant gentleman
were wont to be used to be
forsooth in truth
as idle as she may hang together bored to bits
want lack
weathercock direction pointer (or maybe a reference to feathers in Robin's cap)
dickens devil
a league friendship
goodman husband

Act 3 Scene 2
Windsor: a street

Enter ROBIN, followed by MISTRESS PAGE

MISTRESS PAGE Nay, keep your way, little gallant. You were wont to be a follower, but now you are a leader. Whether had you rather, lead mine eyes, or eye your master's heels?

ROBIN I had rather, forsooth, go before you like a man than follow him like a dwarf.

MISTRESS PAGE O, you are a flattering boy: now I see you'll be a courtier.

[*Enter* FORD]

FORD Well met, Mistress Page. Whither go you?

MISTRESS PAGE Truly, sir, to see your wife. Is she at home?

FORD Ay, and as idle as she may hang together, for want of company. I think if your husbands were dead you two would marry.

MISTRESS PAGE Be sure of that – two other husbands.

FORD Where had you this pretty weathercock?

MISTRESS PAGE I cannot tell what the dickens his name is my husband had him of. What do you call your knight's name, sirrah?

ROBIN Sir John Falstaff.

FORD Sir John Falstaff!

MISTRESS PAGE He, he. I can never hit on's name. There is such a league between my goodman and he! Is your wife at home indeed?

FORD Indeed she is.

MISTRESS PAGE By your leave, sir. I am sick till I see her.

[*Exeunt Robin and Mistress Page*]

Ford thinks the Wives intend to have sex with Falstaff. He plans his neighbours shall see him trap Falstaff and reveal Page as a cuckold. Page supports Slender's wooing of Anne. The Host praises Fenton.

1 **Fevered thoughts** (in groups)

The short sentences, urgent tone and powerful images of Ford's soliloquy (lines 22–36) convey the passionate intensity of his fevered imagination. Obsessed with Falstaff, and suspicious of his wife's fidelity, his mind leaps from thought to thought as he plans what he will do. Share the soliloquy around the group, each person speaking up to a punctuation mark, then handing on to the next. Try hissing some lines, packing them with as much emotional intensity as you can. Afterwards, talk together about the following:

a Just what does Ford intend to do? List his plans.

b What do you think he means by 'torture my wife'?

c *Merry Wives* is a comedy, so it is unlikely that Ford's neighbours will applaud and praise his actions as he claims. What is more likely to happen?

2 Suitors for Anne Page

Page supports Slender as a future son-in-law, but his wife favours Doctor Caius. Now the Host talks of Fenton, and his imagery paints a glowing picture of the young gentleman. Suggest what each image conjures up in your mind:

'He capers, he dances, he has eyes of youth'

'he writes verses, he speaks holiday'

'he smells April and May'

''tis in his buttons' puzzles everybody. It may mean 'it's in his nature'. Make your own guess!

---

point-blank twelve score straight over 240 paces
pieces out encourages
motion and advantage support and opportunity
hear this shower sing in the wind guess trouble's coming
so-seeming outwardly virtuous
Actaeon cuckold (see page 38)
cry aim applaud (like spectators at an archery match)
knot group of folk
stand wholly for whole-heartedly support

FORD Has Page any brains? Hath he any eyes? Hath he any thinking? Sure, they sleep: he hath no use of them. Why, this boy will carry a letter twenty mile as easy as a cannon will shoot point-blank twelve score. He pieces out his wife's inclination. He gives her folly motion and advantage. And now she's going to my wife, and Falstaff's boy with her. A man may hear this shower sing in the wind. And Falstaff's boy with her! Good plots they are laid, and our revolted wives share damnation together. Well, I will take him, then torture my wife, pluck the borrowed veil of modesty from the so-seeming Mistress Page, divulge Page himself for a secure and wilful Actaeon; and to these violent proceedings all my neighbours shall cry aim. [*Clock strikes*] The clock gives me my cue, and my assurance bids me search. There I shall find Falstaff. I shall be rather praised for this than mocked, for it is as positive as the earth is firm that Falstaff is there. I will go.

[*Enter* SHALLOW, PAGE, HOST, SLENDER, CAIUS, EVANS, *and* RUGBY]

SHALLOW, PAGE, etc. Well met, Master Ford.

FORD Trust me, a good knot. I have good cheer at home, and I pray you all go with me.

SHALLOW I must excuse myself, Master Ford.

SLENDER And so must I, sir. We have appointed to dine with Mistress Anne, and I would not break with her for more money than I'll speak of.

SHALLOW We have lingered about a match between Anne Page and my cousin Slender, and this day we shall have our answer.

SLENDER I hope I have your good will, father Page.

PAGE You have, son Slender. I stand wholly for you. But my wife, Master Doctor, is for you altogether.

CAIUS Ay, by gar, and de maid is love-a me; my nursh-a Quickly tell me so mush.

HOST [*To Page*] What say you to young Master Fenton? He capers, he dances, he has eyes of youth, he writes verses, he speaks holiday, he smells April and May. He will carry't, he will carry't; 'tis in his buttons, he will carry't.

Page flatly rejects Fenton as a husband for Anne. If she marries him, Page will give her no money. Ford promises 'sport' at his home, intending to catch Falstaff. The Wives prepare the buck-basket.

1 Links with *King Henry IV*

Fenton is a high-status gentleman, but Page is adamant he shall not wed Anne or get his hands on Page's wealth. Page's antipathy towards Fenton reveals an attitude that was held by some of the Elizabethan middle classes. Although upward social mobility was increasingly common and desired, a wariness existed among wealthy merchants. They thought some of the young noblemen who pursued their daughters did so only to inherit the fathers' hard-earned wealth.

Page's additional reason for rejecting Fenton, 'He kept company with the wild Prince and Poins', links *Merry Wives* securely with Shakespeare's earlier plays *King Henry IV Parts 1* and 2. Falstaff's exploits with the young Prince Hal and his dissolute companion Poins had been hugely successful audience-pullers. Elizabethan audiences would respond with recognition and pleasure to line 56.

Find a copy of *King Henry IV Part 1* and read Act 1 Scene 2 and Act 2 Scene 2 and you will see why Page suspects Fenton – the Prince and Poins plot and carry out a robbery of citizens just like Page!

2 A great buck-basket (in pairs)

Mistress Page and Mistress Ford make their preparations for the humiliation of Falstaff. The buck-basket (basket for dirty linen) is their chosen instrument. Just what have they in mind? Make a guess before you read on. If you already know, suggest how the Wives might behave towards the basket in the opening lines of Scene 3 in order to whet the audience's appetite, anticipating the fun ahead.

---

of no having penniless
substance wealth
simply with no dowry or prospects
anon soon
canary wine (from the Canary Islands)
pipe-wine wine in pipes (casks), and a pun on dancing to a pipe (when Ford's beating makes Falstaff dance to his tune)
brew-house (where beer was made)
whitsters bleachers of linen
Datchet Mead see map on page 164

PAGE Not by my consent, I promise you. The gentleman is of no having. He kept company with the wild Prince and Poins. He is of too high a region; he knows too much. No, he shall not knit a knot in his fortunes with the finger of my substance. If he take her, let him take her simply. The wealth I have waits on my consent, and my consent goes not that way.

FORD I beseech you heartily, some of you go home with me to dinner. Besides your cheer, you shall have sport: I will show you a monster. Master Doctor, you shall go. So shall you, Master Page, and you, Sir Hugh.

SHALLOW Well, fare you well. [*Aside to Slender*] We shall have the freer wooing at Master Page's. [*Exeunt Shallow and Slender*]

CAIUS Go home, John Rugby. I come anon. [*Exit Rugby*]

HOST Farewell, my hearts. I will to my honest knight Falstaff; and drink canary with him. [*Exit*]

FORD [*Aside*] I think I shall drink in pipe-wine first with him; I'll make him dance. – Will you go, gentles?

PAGE, CAIUS, and EVANS Have with you to see this monster.

Exeunt

Act 3 Scene 3
Master Ford's house

Enter MISTRESS FORD and MISTRESS PAGE

MISTRESS FORD What John! What, Robert!

[*Enter John and Robert with a great buck-basket*]

MISTRESS PAGE Quickly, quickly! Is the buck-basket –

MISTRESS FORD I warrant. What, Robin, I say!

MISTRESS PAGE Come, come, come.

MISTRESS FORD Here, set it down.

MISTRESS PAGE Give your men the charge. We must be brief.

MISTRESS FORD Marry, as I told you before, John and Robert, be ready here hard by in the brew-house, and when I suddenly call you, come forth, and without any pause or staggering take this basket on your shoulders. That done, trudge with it in all haste, and carry it among the whitsters in Datchet Mead, and there empty it in the muddy ditch close by the Thames side.

Robin reports Falstaff's arrival. Mistress Page promises to reward Robin for being part of her plot. She hides. Mistress Ford predicts humiliation for Falstaff, who then arrives and woos her.

---

1 Smart or shabby? (in small groups)

Mistress Page's description of Robin suggests that the boy is colourfully dressed. A Jack-a-Lent was a brightly costumed puppet made for a game in the season of Lent (boys threw stones at the puppet). But does Mistress Page's promise of 'a new doublet and hose' suggest that Robin's costume is shabby? Make your suggestions as to how Falstaff is likely to dress his page.

2 The language of theatre

The Wives are about to play-act to deceive Falstaff. Pick out the two theatrical words in lines 28–9. You may like to know that those lines are sometimes described by critics as 'meta-theatre': theatre about theatre, or moments when the language acknowledges the theatrical nature of the play, underlining the artificiality of what is being portrayed.

3 Over the top! (in pairs)

Falstaff and Mistress Ford are both playing games with each other. He is posing as the besotted lover, she is responding as innocently fascinated by him, holding back a little, but obviously greatly attracted. In performance, the two actors usually make the falseness of what is being said quite clear to the audience by delivering the already extravagant language in a patently exaggerated way. He is bombastic and over-romantic, her style is coquettish and flirting.

Take parts and speak lines 33–66 to bring out the absurdity of the episode. Remember: neither character believes a word of what they say to each other!

---

eyas-musket young hawk
turn me away sack me
unwholesome humidity steaming rogue
turtles from jays true wives from false (turtle doves are faithful; jays are noisy and have gaudy plumage)
period climax, achievement
cog lie, flatter
prate speak idly
right arched beauty, ship-tire, tire-valiant, of Venetian admittance see activity 1, page 82

MISTRESS PAGE [*To John and Robert*] You will do it?

MISTRESS FORD I ha' told them over and over, they lack no direction. – Be gone, and come when you are called.

[*Exeunt John and Robert*]

[*Enter* ROBIN]

MISTRESS PAGE Here comes little Robin.

MISTRESS FORD How now, my eyas-musket, what news with you?

ROBIN My master, Sir John, is come in at your back door, Mistress Ford, and requests your company.

MISTRESS PAGE You little Jack-a-Lent, have you been true to us?

ROBIN Ay, I'll be sworn. My master knows not of your being here, and hath threatened to put me into everlasting liberty if I tell you of it; for he swears he'll turn me away.

MISTRESS PAGE Thou'rt a good boy. This secrecy of thine shall be a tailor to thee and shall make thee a new doublet and hose. – I'll go hide me.

MISTRESS FORD Do so. – Go tell thy master I am alone.

[*Exit Robin*]

Mistress Page, remember you your cue.

MISTRESS PAGE I warrant thee. If I do not act it, hiss me. [*Exit*]

MISTRESS FORD Go to, then. - We'll use this unwholesome humidity, this gross watery pumpkin. We'll teach him to know turtles from jays.

[*Enter* FALSTAFF]

FALSTAFF Have I caught thee, my heavenly jewel? Why now let me die, for I have lived long enough. This is the period of my ambition. O this blessèd hour!

MISTRESS FORD O sweet Sir John!

FALSTAFF Mistress Ford, I cannot cog; I cannot prate, Mistress Ford. Now shall I sin in my wish: I would thy husband were dead. I'll speak it before the best lord, I would make thee my lady.

MISTRESS FORD I your lady, Sir John? Alas, I should be a pitiful lady.

FALSTAFF Let the court of France show me such another. I see how thine eye would emulate the diamond. Thou hast the right arched beauty of the brow that becomes the ship-tire, the tire-valiant, or any tire of Venetian admittance.

Falstaff continues to flatter Mistress Ford extravagantly as he protests his love for her. Her replies imply disaster ahead for him. News of Mistress Page's approach makes Falstaff hide behind the arras.

---

1 **Extravagant comparisons** (in small groups)

Falstaff's wooing contains references which make little sense to a modern audience. Talk together about each of the following and decide whether the actors might use gestures and actions to help convey meaning.

Lines 42–4: Falstaff claims that Alice Ford's arched eyebrows delightfully suit ('becomes') elaborate kinds of head-dress ('tire'): the 'ship-tire', shaped like a ship; the 'tire-valiant', another fanciful head-dress; or any head-dress fashionable in Venice ('of Venetian admittance').

Line 49: Falstaff says how dignified Mistress Ford would look in a 'semicircled farthingale': a hooped skirt projecting only at the back.

Line 50: He declares that Nature is Mistress Ford's friend in making her beautiful, but Fortune is her foe in keeping her of modest social status.

Line 60: Asserting that he does not love Mistress Page, Falstaff says he would rather walk past the foul-smelling Counter prison in Southwark.

2 **Irony** (in pairs)

Irony is saying one thing, but meaning another. What does Mistress Ford really have in mind at lines 62–3 and 65–6? Dramatic irony is when a character is not aware of the implications of what he or she says. Identify the dramatic irony in line 64.

---

kerchief headscarf
hawthorn-buds affected young men
Bucklersbury London street where medicinal herbs ('simples') were sold. The herbs made the street smell sweet.
simple-time midsummer, the best time for herbs
ensconce me hide myself
arras tapestry hanging to cover a wall
tattling gossiping

MISTRESS FORD A plain kerchief, Sir John. My brows become nothing else, nor that well neither.

FALSTAFF Thou art a tyrant to say so. Thou wouldst make an absolute courtier, and the firm fixture of thy foot would give an excellent motion to thy gait in a semicircled farthingale. I see what thou wert if Fortune (thy foe) were – not Nature – thy friend. Come, thou canst not hide it.

MISTRESS FORD Believe me, there's no such thing in me.

FALSTAFF What made me love thee? Let that persuade thee. There's something extraordinary in thee. Come, I cannot cog and say thou art this and that, like a many of these lisping hawthorn-buds that come like women in men's apparel and smell like Bucklersbury in simple-time. I cannot. But I love thee, none but thee; and thou deserv'st it.

MISTRESS FORD Do not betray me, sir. I fear you love Mistress Page.

FALSTAFF Thou mightst as well say I love to walk by the Counter gate, which is as hateful to me as the reek of a lime-kiln.

MISTRESS FORD Well, heaven knows how I love you, and you shall one day find it.

FALSTAFF Keep in that mind. I'll deserve it.

MISTRESS FORD Nay, I must tell you, so you do; or else I could not be in that mind.

[*Enter* ROBIN]

ROBIN Mistress Ford, Mistress Ford! Here's Mistress Page at the door, sweating and blowing and looking wildly, and would needs speak with you presently.

FALSTAFF She shall not see me. I will ensconce me behind the arras.

MISTRESS FORD Pray you, do so; she's a very tattling woman.

[*Falstaff stands behind the arras*]

[*Enter* MISTRESS PAGE]

What's the matter? How now?

MISTRESS PAGE O Mistress Ford, what have you done? You're shamed, you're overthrown, you're undone for ever.

MISTRESS FORD What's the matter, good Mistress Page?

The two Wives put on an elaborate show for Falstaff, as Mistress Page tells of Ford's approach. How can Falstaff be got out of the house? The buck-basket provides the solution!

'Let me creep in here.' How would you stage the comic business of Falstaff and the buck-basket between lines 105–11?

well-a-day alas!
undone ruined
clear innocent
friend lover
good life respectability
Bethink you of some conveyance Think of some way of getting him out of the house!
Look, here is a basket Mistress Page's innocent remark should bring the house down!
bucking the washing of dirty linen
whiting-time bleaching time
Datchet Mead see map on page 164

MISTRESS PAGE O well-a-day, Mistress Ford, having an honest man to your husband, to give him such cause of suspicion!

MISTRESS FORD What cause of suspicion?

MISTRESS PAGE What cause of suspicion? Out upon you! How am I mistook in you!

MISTRESS FORD Why, alas, what's the matter?

MISTRESS PAGE Your husband's coming hither, woman, with all the officers in Windsor, to search for a gentleman that he says is here now in the house, by your consent, to take an ill advantage of his absence. You are undone.

MISTRESS FORD 'Tis not so, I hope.

MISTRESS PAGE Pray heaven it be not so that you have such a man here! But 'tis most certain your husband's coming, with half Windsor at his heels, to search for such a one. I come before to tell you. If you know yourself clear, why, I am glad of it; but if you have a friend here, convey, convey him out. Be not amazed, call all your senses to you, defend your reputation, or bid farewell to your good life forever.

MISTRESS FORD What shall I do? There is a gentleman, my dear friend; and I fear not mine own shame so much as his peril. I had rather than a thousand pound he were out of the house.

MISTRESS PAGE For shame, never stand 'you had rather' and 'you had rather'! Your husband's here at hand! Bethink you of some conveyance. In the house you cannot hide him. – O, how have you deceived me! – Look, here is a basket. If he be of any reasonable stature, he may creep in here, and throw foul linen upon him, as if it were going to bucking; or – it is whiting-time – send him by your two men to Datchet Mead.

MISTRESS FORD He's too big to go in there. What shall I do?

[FALSTAFF *rushes out of hiding*]

FALSTAFF Let me see't, let me see't! O, let me see't! I'll in, I'll in! Follow your friend's counsel. I'll in!

MISTRESS PAGE What, Sir John Falstaff! [*Aside to him*] Are these your letters, knight?

FALSTAFF I love thee. Help me away. Let me creep in here. I'll never –

[*Falstaff gets into the basket; they cover him with clothes*]

MISTRESS PAGE [*To Robin*] Help to cover your master, boy. – Call your men, Mistress Ford. – You dissembling knight! [*Exit Robin*]

Ford, obsessed with sexual jealousy, exclaims about cuckoldry ('buck!') but allows the buck-basket to be carried out. Frantic, he orders a search of the house. The Wives enjoy their plot.

---

1 Stage the action! (in groups)

Every production of *Merry Wives* seizes the comic opportunities offered from the entry of John and Robert to the departure of Page and the others to search the house (lines 112–34). All productions use those 23 lines to create a great deal of stage 'business'. Use the suggestions below to work out how you would stage the episode.

John and Robert: What are they doing that makes Mistress Ford exclaim 'Look how you drumble!' (dawdle)? How do they react to Ford's outbursts?

Ford: Think of his emotional state: consumed by jealousy, anger, and a burning desire to catch Falstaff. How might a person in the grip of such extreme emotions behave? Experiment with different ways of speaking each word or short phrase he utters. His fevered repetition of 'buck!' shows that he has only sex in mind: 'buck' means a stag in the rutting season, and the buck's horns symbolised sexual activity and cuckoldry.

Mistress Ford: Just how does she remind Ford that in Elizabethan England the dirty washing is a woman's affair, not for a man to meddle with?

Page, Caius and Evans: How do they regard Ford's frantic behaviour?

Falstaff: Does Falstaff give any sign, undetected by Ford, that he's in the basket? Mistress Page's line 138 suggests he did, and Mistress Ford hints that Falstaff's fear made him lose control of his bowels, and he soiled himself (line 140), so really is in 'need of washing'.

---

cowl-staff pole to carry the basket
season rutting (mating) time for bucks
unkennel the fox drive the fox out of its earth (lair)
stop fox earths were 'stopped' (barred) with stakes
humours troubled emotional states
taking fright (did Falstaff make noises in the basket?)
strain disposition

MISTRESS FORD What, John! Robert! John!

[*Enter* JOHN *and* ROBERT]

Go, take up these clothes here quickly. Where's the cowl-staff? Look how you drumble! [*They fit the cowl-staff*] Carry them to the laundress in Datchet Mead. Quickly, come!

[*Enter* FORD, PAGE, CAIUS, *and* EVANS]

FORD [*To his companions*] Pray you, come near. If I suspect without cause, why then make sport at me, then let me be your jest, I deserve it. – How now? Whither bear you this?

JOHN To the laundress, forsooth.

MISTRESS FORD Why, what have you to do whither they bear it? You were best meddle with buck-washing!

FORD Buck? I would I could wash myself of the buck! Buck, buck, buck! Ay, buck! I warrant you, buck – and of the season too, it shall appear.

[*Exeunt John and Robert with the basket*]

Gentlemen, I have dreamed tonight. I'll tell you my dream. Here, here; here be my keys. Ascend my chambers. Search, seek, find out. I'll warrant we'll unkennel the fox. Let me stop this way first.

[*He locks the door*]

So; now escape.

PAGE Good Master Ford, be contented. You wrong yourself too much.

FORD True, Master Page. – Up, gentlemen, you shall see sport anon. Follow me, gentlemen. [*Exit*]

EVANS This is fery fantastical humours and jealousies.

CAIUS By gar, 'tis no the fashion of France. It is not jealous in France.

PAGE Nay, follow him, gentlemen. See the issue of his search.

[*Exeunt Caius and Evans, followed by Page*]

MISTRESS PAGE Is there not a double excellency in this?

MISTRESS FORD I know not which pleases me better, that my husband is deceived, or Sir John.

MISTRESS PAGE What a taking was he in when your husband asked who was in the basket!

MISTRESS FORD I am half afraid he will have need of washing, so throwing him into the water will do him a benefit.

MISTRESS PAGE Hang him, dishonest rascal! I would all of the same strain were in the same distress.

The Wives think Falstaff's dissolute nature has not been cured. They plan another humiliation for him. Ford, criticised by everyone for his suspicions and behaviour, asks his wife for pardon.

---

1 More medicine for Falstaff (in pairs)

The Wives think that Falstaff needs another dose of harsh medicine to cure his 'dissolute disease'. They plan to send Mistress Quickly to him to excuse the buck-basket humilation, and to say he will have better luck if he comes to Mistress Ford tomorrow at eight.

The image of 'tricks' and 'punishment' as medicine throws light on the nature of drama. It suggests that characters learn from hard experience: that their nature changes for the better. Which other characters in addition to Falstaff do you think also need a dose of comic medicine to help them see things (and themselves) more clearly?

2 What does she mean? (in small groups)

Mistress Page's line 157 has puzzled many people. What does she mean by it? Take turns to step into role as Mistress Page and say what's in your mind as you speak 'Heard you that?'.

3 'Pardon me' (in groups of three)

Ford is subjected to a barrage of criticism from everyone. The other men rally to support Mistress Ford and to chide her husband for thinking ill of her. After some grudging words Ford seems to relent, and in lines 175–8 he asks to be pardoned. He makes his request three times, seemingly with increasing urgency. But the Wives make no reply to his repeated request. Why not?

Take parts as Ford, his wife and Mistress Page. Try out different ways of performing the final four lines opposite. Your task is to show just how the Wives respond to each plea for forgiveness. Afterwards, still in role, talk together about why you behaved as you did.

---

foolish carrion gossiping old woman ('carrion', flesh for scavengers, is not meant contemptuously)
compass carry out
chambers bedrooms
coffers chests
presses cupboards
the day of judgement doomsday (Evans means 'heaven must not pardon my sins')
imagination delusion
distemper foul mood

MISTRESS FORD I think my husband hath some special suspicion of Falstaff's being here, for I never saw him so gross in his jealousy till now.

MISTRESS PAGE I will lay a plot to try that, and we will yet have more tricks with Falstaff. His dissolute disease will scarce obey this medicine.

MISTRESS FORD Shall we send that foolish carrion, Mistress Quickly, to him, and excuse his throwing into the water, and give him another hope, to betray him to another punishment?

MISTRESS PAGE We will do it. Let him be sent for tomorrow eight o'clock, to have amends.

[*Enter* FORD, PAGE, CAIUS, *and* EVANS]

FORD I cannot find him. Maybe the knave bragged of that he could not compass.

MISTRESS PAGE [*Aside to Mistress Ford*] Heard you that?

MISTRESS FORD You use me well, Master Ford, do you?

FORD Ay, I do so.

MISTRESS FORD Heaven make you better than your thoughts!

FORD Amen!

MISTRESS PAGE You do yourself mighty wrong, Master Ford.

FORD Ay, ay, I must bear it.

EVANS If there be anypody in the house, and in the chambers, and in the coffers, and in the presses, heaven forgive my sins at the day of judgement!

CAIUS By gar, nor I too. There is nobodies.

PAGE Fie, fie, Master Ford, are you not ashamed? What spirit, what devil suggests this imagination? I would not ha' your distemper in this kind for the wealth of Windsor Castle.

FORD 'Tis my fault, Master Page. I suffer for it.

EVANS You suffer for a pad conscience. Your wife is as honest a 'omans as I will desires among five thousand, and five hundred too.

CAIUS By gar, I see 'tis an honest woman.

FORD Well, I promised you a dinner. Come, come, walk in the Park. I pray you pardon me. I will hereafter make known to you why I have done this. – Come, wife, come, Mistress Page, I pray you pardon me. Pray heartily pardon me.

Page proposes a bird-shoot. Everyone agrees to join in. Evans and Caius vow revenge on the Host. Fenton tells of Page's objections to him as Anne's suitor. He declares his love is true, not mercenary.

---

1 **Going a-birding – and mispronunciation!** (in pairs)

Page invites everyone to go 'a-birding'. It was a favourite pastime of some middle- or lower-status Elizabethans, and was a type of hunting. A sparrow-hawk was let loose; small birds, frightened by the predator, would seek shelter in a bush where they would be shot by the hunters. Here, Shakespeare uses it as a plot device: it will get Ford out of his house so that Falstaff can visit Mistress Ford. But it also places a gun in Ford's hands! You will discover the outcome in Act 4.

Shakespeare also uses the shooting-party as an opportunity to have Caius mispronounce 'third'. Imagine you are directing the play. What kind of audience response to his mispronunciation would you hope to evoke, and how would you advise the other characters to react?

2 **Another sub-plot: revenge on the Host** (in pairs)

Scene 3 closes with a reminder of another sub-plot: Evans and Caius plan to take revenge on the Host of the Garter for making them seem foolish over the duel. The Welshman and the Frenchman, only recently sworn enemies, are now united. So just how might they speak lines 187–90, and how do they exit? Make your suggestions.

3 **A change to verse**

Scene 4 opens in verse as Fenton tells why Page objects to him as a son-in-law, and tells Anne he loves her for herself, not for her inheritance. On page 180 you can find probable explanations of why Shakespeare switches from prose to verse.

---

gibes sneering insults
turn me to him will I ask him
be thyself choose for yourself
too great of birth of too high status
my state being galled with my expense because I've squandered all my money
bars obstacles
wild societies bad companions
but as a property for your money
speed me make me successful
Albeit even though
stamps in gold stamped gold coins

PAGE [*To Caius and Evans*] Let's go in, gentlemen; but trust me, we'll mock him. [*To Ford, Caius, and Evans*] I do invite you tomorrow morning to my house to breakfast. After, we'll a-birding together. I have a fine hawk for the bush. Shall it be so?

FORD Anything.

EVANS If there is one, I shall make two in the company.

CAIUS If there be one or two, I shall make-a the turd.

FORD Pray you go, Master Page.

[*Exeunt all but Evans and Caius*]

EVANS I pray you now, remembrance tomorrow on the lousy knave mine host.

CAIUS Dat is good, by gar; with all my heart!

EVANS A lousy knave, to have his gibes and his mockeries! *Exeunt*

ACT 3 SCENE 4
Outside Master Page's house

Enter FENTON and ANNE PAGE

FENTON I see I cannot get thy father's love;
Therefore no more turn me to him, sweet Nan.
ANNE Alas, how then?
FENTON Why, thou must be thyself.
He doth object I am too great of birth,
And that, my state being galled with my expense,
I seek to heal it only by his wealth.
Besides these, other bars he lays before me –
My riots past, my wild societies –
And tells me 'tis a thing impossible
I should love thee but as a property.
ANNE Maybe he tells you true.
FENTON No, heaven so speed me in my time to come!
Albeit I will confess thy father's wealth
Was the first motive that I wooed thee, Anne,
Yet, wooing thee, I found thee of more value
Than stamps in gold or sums in sealèd bags.
And 'tis the very riches of thyself
That now I aim at.

Anne's words show her love for Fenton and her dislike of Slender. Slender attempts to woo Anne, but proves an inept lover. Shallow supports Slender, but Anne wants Slender to speak for himself.

---

1 **What will she do?** (in pairs)

Anne loves Fenton, and urges him to try again to win her father over. If he does not succeed, she has something else in mind, and at line 21 she takes Fenton aside to tell him. Make your guess at her plan.

2 **A clumsy lover** (in groups of four)

Take parts as Anne, Slender, Shallow and Quickly, and prepare a performance of lines 22–58. Try to bring out Slender's foolishness in:

a his use of proverbs (see foot of page).

b his misunderstanding of Shallow's words 'thou hadst a father!' ('Remember the brave exploits of your dad!'). Slender interprets it as an opportunity to tell a silly story about his father.

c his misunderstanding of Anne's use of 'will' (see page 94).

3 **Elizabethan England** (see also page 161)

Slender's wooing gives insight into middle-class preoccupations of the time (and shows that Slender is wealthy).

Line 32 – 'three hundred pounds a year': People were judged by their income.

Lines 42–3 – 'under the degree of a squire': Suitable to her social status as wife of a gentleman.

Line 44 – 'jointure': Wealth settled on a wife to provide for her as widow (£150 was a considerable settlement).

---

kinsman relative (Slender)
a shaft or a bolt longbow or crossbow arrows (a proverb: 'I'll try it oneway or the other')
'Slid by God's eyelid
venturing attempting
coz kinsman
maintain keep
cut and long-tail dogs with docked (cut) or undocked tails (a proverb: 'whatever happens')
What is your will? What do you want?

ANNE Gentle Master Fenton,
Yet seek my father's love, still seek it, sir,
If opportunity and humblest suit
Cannot attain it, why then – hark you hither! [*They talk aside*]

[*Enter* SHALLOW, SLENDER, *and* MISTRESS QUICKLY]

SHALLOW Break their talk, Mistress Quickly. My kinsman shall speak for himself.

SLENDER I'll make a shaft or a bolt on't. 'Slid, 'tis but venturing.

SHALLOW Be not dismayed.

SLENDER No, she shall not dismay me. I care not for that, but that I am afeard.

MISTRESS QUICKLY [*To Anne*] Hark ye, Master Slender would speak a word with you.

ANNE I come to him. [*Aside to Fenton*] This is my father's choice.
O, what a world of vile ill-favoured faults
Looks handsome in three hundred pounds a year!

MISTRESS QUICKLY And how does good Master Fenton? Pray you, a word with you.

[*She draws Fenton aside*]

SHALLOW She's coming. To her, coz! O boy, thou hadst a father!

SLENDER I had a father, Mistress Anne; my uncle can tell you good jests of him. – Pray you, uncle, tell Mistress Anne the jest how my father stole two geese out of a pen, good uncle.

SHALLOW Mistress Anne, my cousin loves you.

SLENDER Ay, that I do, as well as I love any woman in Gloucestershire.

SHALLOW He will maintain you like a gentlewoman.

SLENDER Ay, that I will, come cut and long-tail, under the degree of a squire.

SHALLOW He will make you a hundred and fifty pounds jointure.

ANNE Good Master Shallow, let him woo for himself.

SHALLOW Marry, I thank you for it. I thank you for that good comfort. – She calls you, coz. I'll leave you. [*He stands aside*]

ANNE Now, Master Slender.

SLENDER Now, good Mistress Anne.

ANNE What is your will?

Slender shows he cares little for Anne. Page rebukes Fenton, showing he sees Slender as Anne's husband. Fenton asks Mistress Page for support. She promises to favour Anne's own choice of husband.

1 **Another misunderstanding** (in pairs)

Slender shows his stupidity again. Anne asks 'What is your will?' (What do you want?), and interpreting 'will' as meaning making his will, he declares he is healthy. Anne has to explain, and Slender's response (lines 55–8) shows he has no feelings for her. Take turns to speak all Slender's lines opposite to show he is a complete ninny.

2 **Elizabethan patriarchy** (in small groups)

The Merry Wives of Windsor celebrates the independence and intelligence of Elizabethan women. Mistress Ford and Mistress Page prove more than a match for any man. But they live in a patriarchal society where men have virtually all the power (see page 168). That patriarchal power is evident in Page's sharp comment to Fenton: 'my daughter is disposed of'. For all Page's apparent good humour, he regards Anne as a chattel, a thing to be 'disposed of' as he pleases – and that's not to Fenton!

Page is one of many such fathers in Shakespeare's plays: a man who seeks to exercise control over his daughter's life, especially in the choice of the man she marries. Research the following daughters to identify the play in which they appear, the name of each father, and how far their situation resembles that of Anne Page: Desdemona, Hermia, Imogen, Sylvia, Juliet, Cordelia, Jessica, Celia, Hero.

3 **'Bowled to death with turnips'** (in pairs)

Anne is appalled at the thought of being married to Doctor Caius. Invent a few 'rather than's' of your own in the style of lines 79–80.

'Od's heartlings God's little heart
motions proposals
happy man be his dole! good luck to whoever wins you
manners social customs (of not marrying someone from a lower class)
advance the colours of continue to woo (advance with my military flag flying)
set quick i'th'earth buried up to my head
so am I affected I will feel the same way

SLENDER My will? 'Od's heartlings, that's a pretty jest indeed! I ne'er made my will yet, I thank heaven. I am not such a sickly creature, I give heaven praise.

ANNE I mean, Master Slender, what would you with me?

SLENDER Truly, for mine own part, I would little or nothing with you. Your father and my uncle hath made motions. If it be my luck, so; if not, happy man be his dole! They can tell you how things go better than I can.

[*Enter* PAGE *and* MISTRESS PAGE]

You may ask your father; here he comes.

PAGE Now, Master Slender. – Love him, daughter Anne. –
Why, how now? What does Master Fenton here?
You wrong me, sir, thus still to haunt my house.
I told you, sir, my daughter is disposed of.

FENTON Nay, Master Page, be not impatient.

MISTRESS PAGE Good Master Fenton, come not to my child.

PAGE She is no match for you.

FENTON Sir, will you hear me?

PAGE No, good Master Fenton, –
Come, Master Shallow, come, son Slender, in. –
Knowing my mind, you wrong me, Master Fenton.

[*Exeunt Page, Shallow, and Slender*]

MISTRESS QUICKLY Speak to Mistress Page.

FENTON Good Mistress Page, for that I love your daughter
In such a righteous fashion as I do,
Perforce against all checks, rebukes, and manners
I must advance the colours of my love
And not retire. Let me have your good will.

ANNE Good mother, do not marry me to yond fool.

MISTRESS PAGE I mean it not; I seek you a better husband.

MISTRESS QUICKLY That's my master, Master Doctor.

ANNE Alas, I had rather be set quick i'th'earth,
And bowled to death with turnips.

MISTRESS PAGE Come, trouble not yourself. – Good Master Fenton,
I will not be your friend nor enemy.
My daughter will I question how she loves you,
And as I find her, so am I affected.
Till then, farewell, sir. She must needs go in;
Her father will be angry.

[*Exeunt Mistress Page and Anne*]

Mistress Quickly claims she has persuaded Mistress Page to accept Anne's wishes. She will help both Caius and Slender, but favours Fenton. Falstaff grumbles about his ordeal of being tipped into the Thames.

---

1 Wandering loyalties (in pairs)

Mistress Quickly's soliloquy (lines 94–100) shows how her loyalties switch from moment to moment. She first hopes that Caius will win Anne. Then she favours Slender, then Fenton. Practise speaking her lines to show how her thoughts and feelings veer wildly.

2 Search Shakespeare's wastepaper basket! (in pairs)

Scene 5 opens with Falstaff sharing his troubles with the audience. His reflections on how he has been humiliated is rich in imagery. Perhaps Shakespeare wrote a number of different versions of each image, and threw all but one away as he settled on his final preference. Empty out Shakespeare's wastepaper basket! Write one or two different versions that express the same general meaning as each of the following images:

'like a barrow of butcher's offal'.

'I'll have my brains ta'en out and buttered, and give them to a dog for a new year's gift.'

'as little remorse as they would have drowned a blind bitch's puppies, fifteen i'th'litter'.

'as deep as hell'.

'I should have been a mountain of mummy.'

3 Make 'em laugh

How might Falstaff speak lines 9–10, 'And you may know by my size that I have a kind of alacrity in sinking', to make the audience explode with laughter?

---

in sooth in truth
speciously especially
slack neglect
a quart two pints
toast piece of toast (to warm the drink)
offal uneatable meat
The rogues (John and Robert)
slighted me tipped me contemptuously
blind bitch's puppies (new-born puppies are blind)
shelvy sloping
mummy dead flesh

FENTON Farewell, gentle mistress; farewell, Nan.

MISTRESS QUICKLY This is my doing now. 'Nay', said I, 'will you cast away your child on a fool and a physician? Look on Master Fenton.' This is my doing.

FENTON I thank thee, and I pray thee once tonight
Give my sweet Nan this ring. There's for thy pains.

[*He gives her a ring and money*]

MISTRESS QUICKLY Now Heaven send thee good fortune!

[*Exit Fenton*]

A kind heart he hath. A woman would run through fire and water for such a kind heart. But yet I would my master had Mistress Anne; or I would Master Slender had her; or, in sooth, I would Master Fenton had her. I will do what I can for them all three, for so I have promised, and I'll be as good as my word – but speciously for Master Fenton. Well, I must of another errand to Sir John Falstaff from my two mistresses. What a beast am I to slack it!

[*Exit*]

ACT 3 SCENE 5
The Garter Inn

Enter FALSTAFF

FALSTAFF Bardolph, I say!

[*Enter* BARDOLPH]

BARDOLPH Here, sir.

FALSTAFF Go fetch me a quart of sack; put a toast in't.

[*Exit Bardolph*]

Have I lived to be carried in a basket like a barrow of butcher's offal, and to be thrown in the Thames? Well, if I be served such another trick, I'll have my brains ta'en out and buttered, and give them to a dog for a new year's gift. The rogues slighted me into the river with as little remorse as they would have drowned a blind bitch's puppies, fifteen i'th'litter! And you may know by my size that I have a kind of alacrity in sinking. If the bottom were as deep as hell, I should down. I had been drowned but that the shore was shelvy and shallow – a death that I abhor, for the water swells a man, and what a thing should I have been when I had been swelled! I should have been a mountain of mummy.

Falstaff drinks to remove the taste of river water. Mistress Quickly brings Mistress Ford's explanation, apology and invitation to visit her again. Falstaff accepts. He thinks of Brook and his money, and sees him arrive.

'Between nine and ten, sayst thou?' In this modern-dress production, Falstaff feigns indifference, but Mistress Quickly shows she knows he has fallen into the trap. Compare the costumes here with those on page 50.

reins kidneys (associated with lust)
chalices sacred cups, tankards
a pottle four pints
pullet-sperm eggs
take on with rebuke
erection direction (Mistress Quickly's sexual malapropism is ironically echoed by Falstaff)
yearn soften, grieve
his frailty man's moral weakness
my merit Falstaff's determination to visit Mistress Ford in spite of his recent buck-basket suffering

[*Enter* BARDOLPH *with two tankards of sack*]

BARDOLPH Here's Mistress Quickly, sir, to speak with you.

FALSTAFF Come, let me pour in some sack to the Thames water, for my belly's as cold as if I had swallowed snowballs for pills to cool the reins. Call her in.

BARDOLPH Come in, woman.

[*Enter* MISTRESS QUICKLY]

MISTRESS QUICKLY By your leave; I cry you mercy. Give your worship good morrow.

FALSTAFF [*To Bardolph*] Take away these chalices. Go, brew me a pottle of sack finely.

BARDOLPH With eggs, sir?

FALSTAFF Simple of itself. I'll no pullet-sperm in my brewage.

[*Exit Bardolph with the tankards*]

How now?

MISTRESS QUICKLY Marry, sir, I come to your worship from Mistress Ford.

FALSTAFF Mistress Ford? I have had ford enough. I was thrown into the ford. I have my belly full of ford.

MISTRESS QUICKLY Alas, the day, good heart, that was not her fault. She does so take on with her men; they mistook their erection.

FALSTAFF So did I mine, to build upon a foolish woman's promise.

MISTRESS QUICKLY Well, she laments, sir, for it, that it would yearn your heart to see it. Her husband goes this morning a-birding. She desires you once more to come to her, between eight and nine. I must carry her word quickly. She'll make you amends, I warrant you.

FALSTAFF Well, I will visit her. Tell her so. And bid her think what a man is. Let her consider his frailty, and then judge of my merit.

MISTRESS QUICKLY I will tell her.

FALSTAFF Do so. Between nine and ten, sayst thou?

MISTRESS QUICKLY Eight and nine, sir.

FALSTAFF Well, be gone. I will not miss her.

MISTRESS QUICKLY Peace be with you, sir.

[*Exit*]

FALSTAFF I marvel I hear not of Master Brook. He sent me word to stay within. I like his money well. – O, here he comes.

Falstaff tells Brook (the disguised Ford) of his experience at Mistress Ford's: he and she were ready to make love when Ford suddenly arrived. The buck-basket trick came to his rescue, but it stank!

1 What a story! (in pairs)

Take parts as Falstaff and Ford. Prepare a performance of their dialogue (lines 48–109). Use the suggestions below and on page 102.

- Try to express how Falstaff relishes telling his story. He may have suffered, but is determined to re-create his experience as an exciting tale in which he is the central character. He spins out each episode, embroidering each with fanciful language. He piles event on event to give them the quality of a stage play: 'embraced, kissed, protested, and, as it were, spoke the prologue of our comedy'. He gives 'Rammed' (line 72) its sexual meaning, and he lists with disgust the foul-smelling items of the buck-basket. He is a born story-teller, knowing how to build up suspense as he recounts how Ford nearly discovered him.
- Ford's role offers great opportunities for comedy. Think about his position: having to listen to how he failed to catch Falstaff. He had the fat knight at his mercy, but did not know it! In your reactions to Falstaff's story, try to convey a man struggling to control the powerful emotions of rage, chagrin, frustration and growing incredulity as he realises his mistake. For example, 'A buck-basket?' (line 71) may seem to lie flat on the page, but your job is to bring it to comic life as you express in those few words all Ford's conflicting feelings. Think of a similar line in Oscar Wilde's *The Importance of Being Earnest*. Lady Bracknell is astonished to hear that the baby Ernest was found in a handbag. Every Lady Bracknell tries to bring the house down with just two words: 'A handbag?'. Do the same with 'A buck-basket?'.

---

how sped you how did you succeed
ill-favouredly terribly!
determination intention
peaking cornuto creepy cuckold
protested told of our love
thither provoked and instigated brought there stirred up and looking for trouble
distemper foul mood
invention clever idea
distraction agitation
hinds servants

[*Enter* FORD *disguised as Brook*]

FORD God bless you, sir.

FALSTAFF Now, Master Brook, you come to know what hath passed between me and Ford's wife?

FORD That, indeed, Sir John, is my business.

FALSTAFF Master Brook, I will not lie to you. I was at her house the hour she appointed me.

FORD And how sped you, sir?

FALSTAFF Very ill-favouredly, Master Brook.

FORD How so, sir? Did she change her determination?

FALSTAFF No, Master Brook, but the peaking cornuto her husband, Master Brook, dwelling in a continual 'larum of jealousy, comes me in the instant of our encounter, after we had embraced, kissed, protested, and, as it were, spoke the prologue of our comedy; and at his heels a rabble of his companions, thither provoked and instigated by his distemper, and, forsooth, to search his house for his wife's love.

FORD What, while you were there?

FALSTAFF While I was there.

FORD And did he search for you, and could not find you?

FALSTAFF You shall hear. As good luck would have it, comes in one Mistress Page, gives intelligence of Ford's approach, and, in her invention and Ford's wife's distraction, they conveyed me into a buck-basket.

FORD A buck-basket?

FALSTAFF By the Lord, a buck-basket! Rammed me in with foul shirts and smocks, socks, foul stockings, greasy napkins, that, Master Brook, there was the rankest compound of villainous smell that ever offended nostril.

FORD And how long lay you there?

FALSTAFF Nay, you shall hear, Master Brook, what I have suffered to bring this woman to evil for your good. Being thus crammed in the basket, a couple of Ford's knaves, his hinds, were called forth by their mistress to carry me in the name of foul clothes to Datchet Lane. They took me on their shoulders, met the jealous knave their master in the door, who asked them once or twice what they had in their basket. I quaked for fear lest the lunatic knave would have

Falstaff suffered fright and indignity from being crammed in the buck-basket and thrown in the Thames, but is to visit Mistress Ford again. Ford bewails being a cuckold, but vows to catch Falstaff.

1 Falstaff's language

Falstaff's masterly story-telling is aided by:

a *Rhythmical repetition.*
- 'on went he .... away went I'.
- 'first ... next ... and then'.
- 'Think of that ... think of that ... Think of that ... think of that'.

b *Colourful images.*
- 'jealous rotten bell-wether': a ram, with bell tied to neck, which leads a flock of sheep (just as Ford led his friends into the house).
- 'compassed like a good bilbo in the circumference of a peck': bent like a springy sword into a circle ('peck' is an old measure of grain).
- 'a man of continual dissolution and thaw': Falstaff pictures himself melting as if by the action of nature.
- 'I will be thrown into Etna, as I have been into Thames': Falstaff's way of saying he will go through fire and water to seduce Mistress Ford.

2 Ford's soliloquy (in pairs)

Ford's fevered emotions find expression in short exclamatory sentences and phrases. He decides to accept the public humiliation that catching Falstaff will involve: being known as a cuckold. He will search everywhere in his house, and this time Falstaff cannot escape.

Speak lines 110–19 as a frantic conversation, one person reading up to a punctuation mark, the other 'replying' with the next phrase.

held his hand did nothing
kidney constitution (fat)
Dutch dish fatty meal
Etna volcano in Sicily
embassy message
speed succeed
a hole made in your best coat your reputation is ruined
take the lecher catch the sex-maniac
horn-mad a mad cuckold

searched it; but fate, ordaining he should be a cuckold, held his hand. Well, on went he for a search, and away went I for foul clothes. But mark the sequel, Master Brook. I suffered the pangs of three several deaths: first, an intolerable fright to be detected with a jealous rotten bell-wether; next, to be compassed like a good bilbo in the circumference of a peck, hilt to point, heel to head; and then, to be stopped in like a strong distillation with stinking clothes that fretted in their own grease. Think of that – a man of my kidney – think of that – that am as subject to heat as butter, a man of continual dissolution and thaw. It was a miracle to 'scape suffocation. And in the height of this bath, when I was more than half stewed in grease like a Dutch dish, to be thrown into the Thames, and cooled, glowing hot, in that surge, like a horseshoe. Think of that – hissing hot – think of that, Master Brook!

FORD In good sadness, sir, I am sorry that for my sake you have suffered all this. My suit, then, is desperate? You'll undertake her no more?

FALSTAFF Master Brook, I will be thrown into Etna, as I have been into Thames, ere I will leave her thus. Her husband is this morning gone a-birding. I have received from her another embassy of meeting. 'Twixt eight and nine is the hour, Master Brook.

FORD 'Tis past eight already, sir.

FALSTAFF Is it? I will then address me to my appointment. Come to me at your convenient leisure, and you shall know how I speed; and the conclusion shall be crowned with your enjoying her. Adieu. You shall have her, Master Brook; Master Brook, you shall cuckold Ford.

[*Exit*]

FORD Hum! Ha! Is this a vision? Is this a dream? Do I sleep? Master Ford, awake! Awake, Master Ford! There's a hole made in your best coat, Master Ford. This 'tis to be married; this 'tis to have linen and buck-baskets! Well, I will proclaim myself what I am. I will now take the lecher. He is at my house. He cannot 'scape me. 'Tis impossible he should. He cannot creep into a halfpenny purse, nor into a pepperbox. But lest the devil that guides him should aid him, I will search impossible places. Though what I am I cannot avoid, yet to be what I would not shall not make me tame. If I have horns to make one mad, let the proverb go with me – I'll be horn-mad.

[*Exit*]

Looking back at Act 3

Activities for groups or individuals

1 What time of year?

What season of the year is it in Windsor? Many productions suggest it is high summer, and fill the stage with all kinds of games and action to create a sunny atmosphere of Merrie England. But in Scene 1, Page remarks that it is a 'raw rheumatic day'. His comment inspired a famous 'wintry' production of the play (see page 186). What time of year would you choose? Why? Suggest one or two ways in which you would convey the season to the audience (costume, sets, props, and so on).

2 Headlines

There are five scenes in the act. Invent a newspaper headline for each which pithily sums up what happens.

3 Focus on Ford's feelings

Quickly read through all that Ford says in the act, and make a list of each emotion you think he experiences as he speaks. How many can you find? When you have compiled your list, find a partner and (without showing him or her the list) let your face show each emotion in turn. The partner's task is to identify each facial expression.

4 Focus on Falstaff's fantasies

In Scene 5, Falstaff has a soliloquy (lines 4–14), and a long story (lines 52–97 punctuated with questions by Ford). Both are about his buck-basket experience, and both are delivered in his typically vivid style, full of fanciful images. Pick out three or four images that especially appeal to you and use them to illustrate in some way a picture titled 'The buck-basket'.

5 Different viewpoints

Every character in the play has only a partial view of what goes on. Only the audience 'sees' the whole story unfolding. Step into role as either Robin, Mistress Quickly, John or Robert, and write your account of what has happened so far in the play.

True love: Master Fenton and Anne Page.

6 A real-life story?

Talk together about how likely you think it is that Shakespeare based the Fenton–Anne story on the following well-known real-life couple who were the subject of intense gossip around the time the play was written.

> William, Lord Compton came into great wealth at 21, but he kept bad company and spent wildly. He had to sell off the greater part of his estates, and in 1599 was hugely in debt. He made up his mind to marry Elizabeth Spencer. Although she was below him in social status, she was an heiress. Her father was the immensely wealthy Sir John Spencer, a merchant who had once been Lord Mayor of London. He was nicknamed 'rich Spencer', but he also had a reputation of being very mean. Elizabeth was known to have a huge dowry, which would have paid off Compton's debts, but her father was implacably opposed to the marriage, seeing Compton as a fortune hunter. He tried to hide his daughter away, but the two young people proved to be genuinely in love, and ran away to be married. There is even a story that Compton disguised himself as a baker's boy and took Elizabeth away in a bread basket: an anecdote that may have triggered Shakespeare's imagination about the buck-basket.

Mistress Page is on her way to Ford's house to play another trick on Falstaff. She asks Evans to question her son on Latin grammar. Mistress Quickly finds sexual meanings in William's answers.

1 What's it all about? (in groups of four)

Scene 1 opens with five lines concerned with the Falstaff plot. But it then plays out an episode that seems to have no connection with the rest of the play. William's Latin lesson is unrelated to the humiliation of Falstaff, the wooing of Anne Page or the plans of Evans and Caius to take revenge on the Host of the Garter.

So why did Shakespeare write it? Perhaps he saw it as an opportunity to have a laugh at his own schooldays. Day in, day out in his grammar school, William Shakespeare of Stratford, like William Page of Windsor, would have learned by heart all kinds of definitions and rules from the standard textbook of the time, Lily's *A Short Introduction of Grammar*.

Perhaps Shakespeare wanted to provide further light on Mistress Quickly, who persistently gives almost all she hears a sexual interpretation, for example hearing '*Pulcher*' as 'Polecats' (prostitutes). Or perhaps, in a play that is so much about the use and abuse of language (see page 163), Shakespeare provides yet another example of how language can muddle and twist into all kinds of unintended meanings.

a Take parts, and read the scene through. Don't worry if some of it does not make sense: nobody really 'gets it' on first reading. And don't feel you have to understand the precise meaning of the Latin. It is more important to understand that in Evans' pronunciation and Mistress Quickly's misunderstandings, Shakespeare is sending up the formality of the language education of his time.

b When you have read the whole scene, make your suggestions as to why Shakespeare inserted this scene into the play.

---

courageous mad outraged and angry
playing day holiday
profits nothing … book learns nothing at school
accidence rudiments of Latin grammar
numbers types (singular and plural)
'Od's nouns God's wounds (an oath)
tattlings gossip
lend articles (a question in Lily's *Grammar*)

Act 4 Scene 1
Windsor: a street

Enter MISTRESS PAGE, MISTRESS QUICKLY, and WILLIAM

MISTRESS PAGE Is he at Mistress Ford's already, think'st thou?

MISTRESS QUICKLY Sure he is by this, or will be presently. But truly he is very courageous mad about his throwing into the water. Mistress Ford desires you to come suddenly.

MISTRESS PAGE I'll be with her by and by. I'll but bring my young man here to school. Look where his master comes. 'Tis a playing day, I see.

[*Enter* EVANS]

How now, Sir Hugh, no school today?

EVANS No. Master Slender is let the boys leave to play.

MISTRESS QUICKLY Blessing of his heart!

MISTRESS PAGE Sir Hugh, my husband says my son profits nothing in the world at his book. I pray you, ask him some questions in his accidence.

EVANS Come hither, William. Hold up your head. Come.

MISTRESS PAGE Come on, sirrah. Hold up your head. Answer your master, be not afraid.

EVANS William, how many numbers is in nouns?

WILLIAM Two.

MISTRESS QUICKLY Truly, I thought there had been one number more, because they say ''Od's nouns'.

EVANS Peace your tattlings! – What is 'fair', William?

WILLIAM *Pulcher*.

MISTRESS QUICKLY Polecats? There are fairer things than polecats, sure.

EVANS You are a very simplicity 'oman. I pray you peace. – What is *lapis*, William?

WILLIAM A stone.

EVANS And what is 'a stone', William?

WILLIAM A pebble.

EVANS No, it is *lapis*. I pray you remember in your prain.

WILLIAM *Lapis*.

EVANS That is a good William. What is he, William, that does lend articles?

Evans continues to test William's knowledge of Latin, and Mistress Quickly continues to find sexual meanings in nearly all she hears. Evans rebukes her. Mistress Page is impressed by her son's performance.

---

1 Making sense? (in groups of four)

Use the following to help you prepare a performance of Scene 1.

Lines 34–5: William has learned by heart this definition from his textbook: Lily's *Grammar*.

Line 41: Mistress Quickly is probably thinking of the proverb 'A hog is not bacon until it is hung'.

Lines 45–6: Evans' pronunciation of 'vocative' sets Mistress Quickly thinking of sexual intercourse, and she hears 'caret' as 'carrot', which was an Elizabethan slang word for penis, as was 'root'.

Lines 49–54: She turns 'Genitive case' into 'Jenny's case', a prostitute's vagina, and hears '*horum*' as 'whore'.

Line 56: In Mistress Quickly's mind, 'to hic and to hac' probably means to drink and to whore.

You can find a picture of Mistress Quickly's reaction to Evans' Latin lesson on page 138.

2 Young William

William is the son of Mistress Page. In Shakespeare's day, he would probably have been played by the youngest member of Shakespeare's acting company. Step into role as the actor who originally played William and write your account of the play's first performance at court before Queen Elizabeth I.

---

prabbles silly chatter
Vengeance of a plague on
preeches breeched, beaten on bare buttocks
sprag lively

WILLIAM Articles are borrowed of the pronoun, and be thus declined: *Singulariter, nominativo, hic, haec, hoc.*

EVANS *Nominativo, hig, hag, hog.* Pray you mark: *genitivo, huius.* Well, what is your accusative case?

WILLIAM *Accusativo, hinc.*

EVANS I pray you have your remembrance, child. *Accusativo, hung, hang, hog.*

MISTRESS QUICKLY 'Hang-hog' is Latin for bacon, I warrant you.

EVANS Leave your prabbles, 'oman. – What is the focative case, William?

WILLIAM O – *vocativo* – O.

EVANS Remember, William: focative is *caret.*

MISTRESS QUICKLY And that's a good root.

EVANS 'Oman, forbear.

MISTRESS PAGE Peace!

EVANS What is your genitive case plural, William?

WILLIAM Genitive case?

EVANS Ay.

WILLIAM *Genitivo, horum, harum, horum.*

MISTRESS QUICKLY Vengeance of Jenny's case! Fie on her! Never name her, child, if she be a whore.

EVANS For shame, 'oman!

MISTRESS QUICKLY You do ill to teach the child such words. He teaches him to hic and to hac, which they'll do fast enough of themselves, and to call 'horum'. Fie upon you!

EVANS 'Oman, art thou lunatics? Hast thou no understandings for thy cases, and the numbers of the genders? Thou art as foolish Christian creatures as I would desires.

MISTRESS PAGE [*To Mistress Quickly*] Prithee hold thy peace.

EVANS Show me now, William, some declensions of your pronouns.

WILLIAM Forsooth, I have forgot.

EVANS It is *qui, que, quod.* If you forget your *quis*, your *ques*, and your *quods*, you must be preeches. Go your ways and play, go.

MISTRESS PAGE He is a better scholar than I thought he was.

EVANS He is a good sprag memory. Farewell, Mistress Page.

MISTRESS PAGE Adieu, good Sir Hugh.

[*Exit Evans*]

Get you home, boy.

[*Exit William*]

Come, we stay too long.

Exeunt

Falstaff says that Mistress Ford's sorrow and love have precisely compensated for his suffering. He hides from Mistress Page who reports that Ford is approaching, suspicious that Falstaff is again in the house.

---

1 **From pomposity to anxiety** (in pairs)

Mistress Ford has been talking to Falstaff before they enter, expressing her sorrow for the indignities put upon him, and reassuring him of her love. Falstaff's language accepting what she has said is elaborately formal and courteous. For example, he accepts that her sorrow and love have quite made amends for his suffering 'in all the accoutrement, complement, and ceremony of it' (with all the accompanying formalities).

But in his final sentence Falstaff completely changes his tone as he anxiously enquires if Ford is indeed absent. Practise speaking his lines to make the contrast between his two moods as clear as you can. On stage, his final sentence should make the audience laugh.

2 **Concealment, overhearing and exaggeration** (in pairs)

Mistress Ford invites Falstaff to 'Step into the chamber'. On the open Globe stage, Falstaff probably just stepped behind one of the stage pillars, but he may hide behind the arras (hanging tapestry) as he did in Act 3 Scene 3. It greatly adds to the comedy if the audience can see Falstaff's reactions to all he hears.

Mistress Ford tells Mistress Page to 'Speak louder' to ensure that Falstaff can hear. Throughout their dialogue in lines 9–36 the Wives not only speak up, but also load their voices with exaggerated emotion for Falstaff's benefit, and for audience enjoyment. Speak these lines in ways which will increasingly make Falstaff shake in his shoes! For example, notice how Mistress Page repeats 'I am glad the fat knight is not here' to make him quake.

---

hath eaten up my sufferance has made up for my suffering
obsequious devoted
profess requital to a hair's breadth accept amends are exactly made
gossip friend
in his old lines playing his old tricks
Eve's daughters women
'Peer out' (Ford speaks to the cuckold's horns he feels on his forehead)
experiment test

Act 4 Scene 2
Master Ford's house

John and Robert carry in the buck-basket.
They leave, and FALSTAFF and MISTRESS FORD enter

FALSTAFF Mistress Ford, your sorrow hath eaten up my sufferance. I see you are obsequious in your love, and I profess requital to a hair's breadth, not only, Mistress Ford, in the simple office of love, but in all the accoutrement, complement, and ceremony of it. But are you sure of your husband now?

MISTRESS FORD He's a-birding, sweet Sir John.

MISTRESS PAGE [*Within*] What ho, gossip Ford! What ho!

MISTRESS FORD Step into the chamber, Sir John.

[*Exit Falstaff*]

[*Enter* MISTRESS PAGE]

MISTRESS PAGE How now, sweetheart, who's at home besides yourself?

MISTRESS FORD Why, none but mine own people.

MISTRESS PAGE Indeed?

MISTRESS FORD No, certainly. [*Aside to her*] Speak louder.

MISTRESS PAGE Truly, I am so glad you have nobody here.

MISTRESS FORD Why?

MISTRESS PAGE Why, woman, your husband is in his old lines again. He so takes on yonder with my husband, so rails against all married mankind, so curses all Eve's daughters of what complexion soever, and so buffets himself on the forehead, crying 'Peer out, peer out!', that any madness I ever yet beheld seemed but tameness, civility, and patience to this his distemper he is in now. I am glad the fat knight is not here.

MISTRESS FORD Why, does he talk of him?

MISTRESS PAGE Of none but him, and swears he was carried out, the last time he searched for him, in a basket; protests to my husband he is now here, and hath drawn him and the rest of their company from their sport to make another experiment of his suspicion. But I am glad the knight is not here. Now he shall see his own foolery.

MISTRESS FORD How near is he, Mistress Page?

The Wives simulate alarm and dismay at Ford's approach. Their pretence fools Falstaff who desperately wishes to escape. The Wives fuel his anxiety and finally propose he disguise himself as a woman.

1 **Director's notes** (in groups of three)

Use the following notes to help you act out lines 31–68.

- The Merry Wives put on a show, with Mistress Ford exclaiming she is 'undone' and Mistress Page loudly rebuking her. Mistress Page makes sure that Falstaff really hears the word 'murder'. It frightens the life out of him. Mistress Ford flutters about pretending she doesn't know how to hide him. But she suddenly pauses then says 'Shall I put him into the basket again?'
- Falstaff reacts as if he's had an electric shock. He positively explodes on to the stage with a gigantic 'No'. You'll get a laugh at that, and then another as after a pause he says 'I'll come no more i'th' basket'.
- From here on it's downhill all the way for Falstaff. The Wives torment him as they close down every avenue of escape. He's constantly on the move, heading towards the door, the chimney and the kiln-hole (oven).
- But he's thwarted at every turn as the Wives pull him up short with a dire warning. He's halfway into the chimney before Mistress Ford makes her remark about the birders firing their guns up it. Mistress Ford increases his agony by counting out on her fingers that long list of where Ford will search: 'press, coffer, chest, trunk, well, vault'.
- So he's in a fit state to respond to Mistress Page's suggestion he goes out 'disguised'. He runs, or rather staggers off, pulling off his jacket and looking both frightened and grateful!

anon very soon
kiln-hole oven
press clothes cupboard
coffer chest for valuables
abstract for the remembrance reminder list
in your own semblance as yourself
muffler scarf
kerchief linen under-hat
extremity course of action
mischief harm, calamity
thrummed fringed

MISTRESS PAGE Hard by, at street end. He will be here anon.

MISTRESS FORD I am undone. The knight is here.

MISTRESS PAGE Why then you are utterly shamed, and he's but a dead man. What a woman are you! Away with him, away with him! Better shame than murder.

MISTRESS FORD Which way should he go? How should I bestow him? Shall I put him into the basket again?

[*Enter* FALSTAFF]

FALSTAFF No, I'll come no more i'th' basket. May I not go out ere he come?

MISTRESS PAGE Alas, three of Master Ford's brothers watch the door with pistols, that none shall issue out; otherwise you might slip away ere he came. But what make you here?

FALSTAFF What shall I do? I'll creep up into the chimney.

MISTRESS FORD There they always use to discharge their birding-pieces.

MISTRESS PAGE Creep into the kiln-hole.

FALSTAFF Where is it?

MISTRESS FORD He will seek there, on my word. Neither press, coffer, chest, trunk, well, vault, but he hath an abstract for the remembrance of such places, and goes to them by his note. There is no hiding you in the house.

FALSTAFF I'll go out, then.

MISTRESS PAGE If you go out in your own semblance, you die, Sir John – unless you go out disguised.

MISTRESS FORD How might we disguise him?

MISTRESS PAGE Alas the day, I know not. There is no woman's gown big enough for him; otherwise he might put on a hat, a muffler, and a kerchief, and so escape.

FALSTAFF Good hearts, devise something; any extremity rather than a mischief.

MISTRESS FORD My maid's aunt, the fat woman of Brentford, has a gown above.

MISTRESS PAGE On my word, it will serve him. She's as big as he is; and there's her thrummed hat and her muffler too. – Run up, Sir John.

MISTRESS FORD Go, go, sweet Sir John! Mistress Page and I will look some linen for your head.

MISTRESS PAGE Quick, quick! We'll come dress you straight. Put on the gown the while. [*Exit Falstaff*]

The Wives hope that Ford's detestation of the fat woman of Brentford will result in Falstaff being beaten. Mistress Page's rhyme asserts their virtue. Ford reacts explosively to the sight of the buck-basket.

1 Who is the fat woman? (in small groups)

The Wives leave to dress Falstaff as the fat woman of Brentford. Who is she? All kinds of guesses have been made, but many scholars think Shakespeare found her in a rude poem, *Jyl of Breyntford's Testament* by Robert Copland, published around 1560. But no one can really be certain, so let your imaginations run and make your own suggestion as to who she is and what she has done that so angers Ford.

2 We are not demure hypocrites! (in pairs)

Mistress Page's two rhyming couplets in lines 85–8 could well stand as an epilogue to the play (and has indeed been spoken at the end in a few productions). It asserts that Wives may be 'merry and yet honest too' (fun-loving yet virtuous and chaste). They may get up to all kinds of tricks, but they do not sleep around ('We do not act'). The final line expresses an Elizabethan proverb: the quiet pig eats all the swill (it's the ones who don't laugh who act immorally). Make up a similar line, using imagery from today's world, that makes the same statement.

3 The buck-basket again! (in pairs)

The sight of the buck-basket is like a red rag to a bull to Ford. He probably does a double-take as he sees it, and he shouts a command 'Set down the basket, villain', then explodes like a firework in a series of short sentences. One person speaks all he says opposite, pausing after each sentence. In the pause, your partner identifies to whom the sentence is addressed and says what Ford has in mind.

shape disguise
good sadness all seriousness
intelligence information
presently immediately
hard at door just outside
as lief rather
panderly rascals villainous pimps
knot, ging, pack band, gang, plotters

MISTRESS FORD I would my husband would meet him in this shape. He cannot abide the old woman of Brentford. He swears she's a witch, forbade her my house, and hath threatened to beat her.

MISTRESS PAGE Heaven guide him to thy husband's cudgel, and the devil guide his cudgel afterwards!

MISTRESS FORD But is my husband coming?

MISTRESS PAGE Ay, in good sadness is he, and talks of the basket too, howsoever he hath had intelligence.

MISTRESS FORD We'll try that; for I'll appoint my men to carry the basket again, to meet him at the door with it as they did last time.

MISTRESS PAGE Nay, but he'll be here presently. Let's go dress him like the witch of Brentford.

MISTRESS FORD I'll first direct my men what they shall do with the basket. Go up; I'll bring linen for him straight. [*Exit*]

MISTRESS PAGE Hang him, dishonest varlet! We cannot misuse him enough.

We'll leave a proof, by that which we will do,
Wives may be merry and yet honest too.
We do not act that often jest and laugh;
'Tis old but true: 'Still swine eats all the draff.' [*Exit*]

[*Enter* MISTRESS FORD, JOHN, *and* ROBERT]

MISTRESS FORD Go, sirs, take the basket again on your shoulders. Your master is hard at door. If he bid you set it down, obey him. Quickly, dispatch! [*Exit*]

JOHN Come, come, take it up.

ROBERT Pray heaven it be not full of knight again!

JOHN I hope not. I had as lief bear so much lead.

[*John and Robert lift the basket*]

[*Enter* FORD, PAGE, SHALLOW, CAIUS, *and* EVANS]

FORD Ay, but if it prove true, Master Page, have you any way then to unfool me again? – Set down the basket, villain!

[*John and Robert set down the basket*]

Somebody call my wife. Youth in a basket! O you panderly rascals! There's a knot, a ging, a pack, a conspiracy against me. Now shall the devil be shamed. – What, wife, I say! Come, come forth! Behold what honest clothes you send forth to bleaching!

Page and the others are amazed by Ford's extreme behaviour. Ford mocks his wife's virtue. He finds no one in the buck-basket, but, still suspicious, asks the others to search the house with him.

---

1 This beats everything! (I) (in small groups)

Ford, Evans and Shallow are dumbfounded by Ford's outbursts. Page warns him that if he continues he will be tied up like a madman (part of the conventional treatment of mentally disturbed persons in Shakespeare's time). Suggest how Ford might have behaved from line 95 to provoke Page's comment 'this passes' (this goes beyond all bounds!).

2 This beats everything! (II) (in small groups)

Every new production of the play must decide just what Ford does with the buck-basket. In one production, he frenetically emptied it piece by piece, flinging the dirty garments all over the stage. He climbed into the basket to complete the task, but then, although it was obvious the basket was empty, he ordered the amazed John and Robert to empty it. They turned it over and shook it vigorously. Even then Ford was not satisfied, and he disappeared into the basket again, only to emerge saying plaintively 'Well, he's not here I seek for' (line 129). Still not satisfied, he carried out another inspection of the basket as it was carried out at line 135.

Work out your own version of just what Ford does with the basket in the episode opposite.

3 This beats everything! (III) (in pairs)

Step into role as John and Robert. Create the conversation they have in the bar of Windsor's Garter Inn that night about their experience at Master Ford's house.

---

hold it out continue your deceit
take up your wife's clothes Evans' strange English creates an unfortunate sexual image
flea's death (anyone you find will be tiny!)
fidelity honour
show no colour for my extremity admit no excuse for my wild actions
table-sport laughing stock, mocked at meals
leman lover

PAGE Why, this passes, Master Ford. You are not to go loose any longer, you must be pinioned.
EVANS Why, this is lunatics. This is mad as a mad dog.
SHALLOW Indeed, Master Ford, this is not well, indeed.
FORD So say I too, sir!

[*Enter* MISTRESS FORD]

Come hither, Mistress Ford! Mistress Ford the honest woman, the modest wife, the virtuous creature, that hath the jealous fool to her husband! I suspect without cause, mistress, do I?
MISTRESS FORD Heaven be my witness you do, if you suspect me in any dishonesty.
FORD Well said, brazen-face, hold it out. – Come forth, sirrah!

[*He opens the basket and begins pulling out clothes*]

PAGE This passes!
MISTRESS FORD Are you not ashamed? Let the clothes alone.
FORD I shall find you anon.
EVANS 'Tis unreasonable. Will you take up your wife's clothes? Come, away.
FORD [*To John and Robert*] Empty the basket, I say!
PAGE Why, man, why?
FORD Master Page, as I am a man, there was one conveyed out of my house yesterday in this basket. Why may not he be there again? In my house I am sure he is. My intelligence is true, my jealousy is reasonable. [*To John and Robert*] Pluck me out all the linen.
MISTRESS FORD If you find a man there, he shall die a flea's death.

[*John and Robert empty the basket*]

PAGE Here's no man.
SHALLOW By my fidelity, this is not well, Master Ford. This wrongs you.
EVANS Master Ford, you must pray, and not follow the imaginations of your own heart. This is jealousies.
FORD Well, he's not here I seek for.
PAGE No, nor nowhere else but in your brain.
FORD Help to search my house this one time. If I find not what I seek, show no colour for my extremity. Let me for ever be your table-sport. Let them say of me, 'As jealous as Ford, that searched a hollow walnut for his wife's leman'. Satisfy me once more. Once more search with me.

[*John and Robert refill the basket and carry it out*]

Ford rants at the fat woman, accuses her of all kinds of trickery and beats her. Evans sees through Falstaff's disguise. Ford, dejected, leaves. Mistress Ford wonders if Falstaff has had sufficient punishment.

'I'll pratt her.' For Elizabethans, 'pratt' could mean to beat on the buttocks. Falstaff pays the penalty for disguising himself as the fat woman of Brentford. How would you stage the episode of the beating?

1 Does Evans detect Falstaff? (in pairs)

Does Evans know (or suspect) that it is Falstaff in disguise when he says the fat lady has 'a great peard' (beard)? Talk together about how you think Evans should deliver his lines 157–9 for maximum comic effect.

cozening quean cheating whore
by the figure using horoscopes
daubery trickery
element understanding
runnion scruffy tart
conjure bewitch
cry out thus upon no trail bark like a hound on a false scent
open give tongue (another hunting term meaning 'to bark')
humour moods
hallowed blessed

MISTRESS FORD What ho, Mistress Page! Come you and the old woman down. My husband will come into the chamber.

FORD Old woman? What old woman's that?

MISTRESS FORD Why, it is my maid's aunt of Brentford.

FORD A witch, a quean, an old cozening quean! Have I not forbid her my house? She comes of errands, does she? We are simple men; we do not know what's brought to pass under the profession of fortune-telling. She works by charms, by spells, by the figure, and such daubery as this is, beyond our element; we know nothing. [*He takes a cudgel*] Come down, you witch, you hag, you! Come down, I say!

MISTRESS FORD Nay, good sweet husband! – Good gentlemen, let him not strike the old woman.

MISTRESS PAGE [*Within*] Come, mother Pratt; come, give me your hand.

FORD I'll pratt her.

[*Enter* MISTRESS PAGE *leading Falstaff disguised as an old woman*]

[*Ford beats Falstaff*]

Out of my door, you witch, you rag, you baggage, you polecat, you runnion! Out, out! I'll conjure you, I'll fortune-tell you!

[*Exit Falstaff*]

MISTRESS PAGE Are you not ashamed? I think you have killed the poor woman.

MISTRESS FORD Nay, he will do it. – 'Tis a goodly credit for you.

FORD Hang her, witch!

EVANS By yea and no, I think the 'oman is a witch indeed. I like not when a 'oman has a great peard. I spy a great peard under her muffler.

FORD Will you follow, gentlemen? I beseech you, follow. See but the issue of my jealousy. If I cry out thus upon no trail, never trust me when I open again.

PAGE Let's obey his humour a little further. Come gentlemen.

[*Exeunt Ford, Page, Shallow, Caius, and Evans*]

MISTRESS PAGE Trust me, he beat him most pitifully.

MISTRESS FORD Nay, by the mass, that he did not: he beat him most unpitifully, methought.

MISTRESS PAGE I'll have the cudgel hallowed and hung o'er the altar. It hath done meritorious service.

MISTRESS FORD What think you? May we, with the warrant of womanhood and the witness of a good conscience, pursue him with any further revenge?

The Wives think Falstaff has learned his lesson. They will tell all to their husbands and ask them to decide if Falstaff deserves further punishment. The Host plans to overcharge the German visitors.

1 **Legal language** (in groups of three or more)

Mistress Page speaks as if Falstaff has undergone an exorcism: the devil of lust ('the spirit of wantonness') has been driven out of him. She then uses Elizabethan legal imagery: unless the devil has complete possession ('fee-simple') of Falstaff, fully protected by law ('with fine and recovery'), he will not do unlawful damage ('in the way of waste') by attempting to seduce the Wives again.

Hardly anyone in an audience today is likely to know the precise meaning of Mistress Ford's legal imagery. Imagine you are a group of actors preparing for performance. Some want to cut the technical legal language, others to modernise it, others to leave it as it is. Conduct your debate!

2 **Into the smithy!** (in groups of three or more)

The Wives agree that if their husbands think that Falstaff should be humiliated again, they, the Wives, should be the main actors ('ministers') in the plot. Mistress Page seems to already have in mind an idea for Falstaff's shaming. In lines 183–4, she uses imagery from an Elizabethan smithy ('forge') where metal was heated, beaten into shape, then cooled in water. Talk together about whether you think modern audiences will 'get' Mistress Page's meaning here more easily than her legal imagery in activity 1 above.

3 **Another plot**

In Scene 3, the plot of Evans and Caius against the Host is put into action. It seems that some German visitors have booked rooms at the Garter. The Host has turned away other guests because he intends to overcharge the foreigners. You can find how the plot works out on page 130.

figures fantasies
further afflicted punished more
ministers agents
period to the jest full stop, conclusion of the trick on Falstaff
the German (an invention of Evans and Caius)
sauce excessively overcharge them
come off pay up

MISTRESS PAGE The spirit of wantonness is sure scared out of him. If the devil have him not in fee-simple, with fine and recovery, he will never, I think, in the way of waste attempt us again.

MISTRESS FORD Shall we tell our husbands how we have served him?

MISTRESS PAGE Yes, by all means, if it be but to scrape the figures out of your husband's brains. If they can find in their hearts the poor unvirtuous fat knight shall be any further afflicted, we two will still be the ministers.

MISTRESS FORD I'll warrant they'll have him publicly shamed, and methinks there would be no period to the jest should he not be publicly shamed.

MISTRESS PAGE Come, to the forge with it, then shape it. I would not have things cool.

Exeunt

Act 4 Scene 3
The Garter Inn

Enter HOST and BARDOLPH

BARDOLPH Sir, the German desires to have three of your horses. The Duke himself will be tomorrow at court, and they are going to meet him.

HOST What duke should that be comes so secretly? I hear not of him in the court. Let me speak with the gentlemen. They speak English?

BARDOLPH Ay, sir. I'll call him to you.

HOST They shall have my horses, but I'll make them pay; I'll sauce them. They have had my house a week at command. I have turned away my other guests. They must come off; I'll sauce them. Come.

Exeunt

Falstaff's trickery is exposed, and Ford apologises to his wife. Page rebukes Ford's extreme comparisons. The men doubt Falstaff will risk a third humiliation, but the Wives are confident they can lure him to the Park.

---

1 Dramatic construction (in small groups)

Scene 4 opens in the middle of a conversation. The Wives have told their stories to their husbands: they decided to humiliate Falstaff for presuming they could be seduced and for sending them identical love letters. They have proposed to play one more trick on Falstaff, luring him to Windsor Great Park at midnight.

Shakespeare has chosen not to show the Wives' explanation to their husbands. Why not? One person steps into role as Shakespeare and gives his reasons. Can 'Shakespeare' persuade the rest of the group that there are good dramatic reasons for not showing the episode?

2 Extreme submission (in small groups)

Ford apologises to his wife for his jealous suspicions. Page suggests that Ford's 'submission' to his wife is close to being as extreme as his previous wild behaviour. Is Page's criticism prompted by what Ford does, or by what he says?

a Suggest and demonstrate actions Ford might make as he speaks lines 5–9. Are those actions likely to provoke Page's rebuke?

b How extreme do you find Ford's two comparisons? Do they seem over-the-top in this play?

c The imagery in lines 7–9 ('Now doth thy honour … faith') is drawn from religion. Ford was once a disbeliever ('heretic'), but now his belief in his wife's virtue is unshakeable ('As firm as faith'). Try inventing another statement of Ford's new-found conviction using different imagery.

'Tis one of the best discretions of a 'oman this is as fine female modesty (or trickery)
at an instant at the same time
wantonness sexual misbehaviour
of late recently
Be not as extreme … offence don't overdo it (as you did your jealousy)
take him trick Falstaff
Devise work out, plan

ACT 4 SCENE 4
Master Ford's house

Enter PAGE, FORD, MISTRESS PAGE, MISTRESS FORD, and EVANS

EVANS 'Tis one of the best discretions of a 'oman as ever I did look upon.

PAGE And did he send you both these letters at an instant?

MISTRESS PAGE Within a quarter of an hour.

FORD Pardon me, wife. Henceforth do what thou wilt.
I rather will suspect the sun with cold
Than thee with wantonness. Now doth thy honour stand
In him that was of late an heretic,
As firm as faith.

PAGE 'Tis well, 'tis well. No more.
Be not as extreme in submission as in offence.
But let our plot go forward. Let our wives
Yet once again, to make us public sport,
Appoint a meeting with this old fat fellow,
Where we may take him and disgrace him for it.

FORD There is no better way than that they spoke of.

PAGE How? To send him word they'll meet him in the Park at midnight? Fie, fie, he'll never come.

EVANS You say he has been thrown in the rivers, and has been grievously peaten as an old 'oman. Methinks there should be terrors in him, that he should not come. Methinks his flesh is punished; he shall have no desires.

PAGE So think I too.

MISTRESS FORD Devise but how you'll use him when he comes,
And let us two devise to bring him thither.

Mistress Page tells the old story of Herne the Hunter. The Wives propose that they meet Falstaff disguised as Herne, and that children, disguised as fairies, rush out at Falstaff and pinch him soundly.

---

1 Telling the tale (in small groups)

Mistress Page's tale of Herne the Hunter (lines 25–35) is wonderfully atmospheric. Shakespeare writes it in verse, perhaps to add to its other-worldly feel, in contrast to the prose of workaday Windsor. It provides excellent opportunities for choral speaking, so prepare your group version of it to deliver to the class.

Share out the lines in any way you think is suitable, some might be spoken by the whole group, some by individuals. Some phrases might be repeated as a refrain (for example, 'Herne the Hunter'), and you can add sound effects (for example, the rattling chain) and actions (Herne 'blasts the trees'. How?). Try to bring out the archaic, fairy-tale quality of the lines: it's there in the words, the phrasing and the rhythms of Mistress Page's narrative.

2 Another cunning plan! (in small groups)

In lines 39–40 and 45–62, the Wives set out their plan for yet another humiliation of Falstaff.

a Sit together in a small circle and speak the lines around the group like a confidential conversation. Each person speaks a short extract that makes sense, then hands on to the next person.

b One person reads the plan slowly, a short section at a time. The rest of the group create actions to illustrate each section.

c One person outlines the plan from memory. The others fill in details they think have been overlooked.

d One person volunteers to outline the plan – but without words!

Herne the Hunter see page 139
Sometime in olden days
takes bewitches
milch-kine dairy cattle
idle-headed eld foolish people of olden times
there want not many there are plenty of
urchins, oafs goblins, elves
waxen tapers candles
diffusèd song wild singing
shape profane unholy disguise
supposèd pretend

MISTRESS PAGE There is an old tale goes that Herne the Hunter,
Sometime a keeper here in Windsor Forest,
Doth all the winter-time, at still midnight,
Walk round about an oak, with great ragg'd horns;
And there he blasts the trees, and takes the cattle,
And makes milch-kine yield blood, and shakes a chain
In a most hideous and dreadful manner.
You have heard of such a spirit, and well you know
The superstitious idle-headed eld
Received and did deliver to our age
This tale of Herne the Hunter for a truth.
PAGE Why, yet there want not many that do fear
In deep of night to walk by this Herne's oak.
But what of this?
MISTRESS FORD Marry, this is our device:
That Falstaff at that oak shall meet with us,
Disguised like Herne, with huge horns on his head.
PAGE Well, let it not be doubted but he'll come;
And in this shape when you have brought him thither,
What shall be done with him? What is your plot?
MISTRESS PAGE That likewise have we thought upon, and thus:
Nan Page my daughter, and my little son,
And three or four more of their growth we'll dress
Like urchins, oafs, and fairies, green and white,
With rounds of waxen tapers on their heads,
And rattles in their hands. Upon a sudden,
As Falstaff, she, and I are newly met,
Let them from forth a sawpit rush at once
With some diffusèd song. Upon their sight,
We two in great amazedness will fly.
Then let them all encircle him about,
And fairy-like to pinch the unclean knight,
And ask him why, that hour of fairy revel,
In their so sacred paths he dares to tread
In shape profane.
MISTRESS FORD And till he tell the truth,
Let the supposèd fairies pinch him sound
And burn him with their tapers.

The plot to mock Falstaff is laid. Evans promises to teach the children what to do. Ford will visit Falstaff as Brook. Page and Mistress Page intend different husbands for Anne.

1 Final humiliation? (in small groups)

Mistress Page's plan includes a final humiliation for Falstaff: 'dis-horn the spirit'. Some critics have argued that the action means much more than removing the horns from Falstaff's head. It will represent taking away his sexual potency, a kind of symbolic castration. Perhaps Elizabethans also saw it in that way, but this may be a case of over-interpretation, where critics read more into the script than may be there.

What do you think? Talk together about lines 60–2 to discover if you think the greater humiliation for Falstaff is in his public mocking by everyone, or in the sexual interpretation of 'dis-horn'.

2 Vizards, properties and tricking (in pairs)

The plot calls for theatrical resources. 'Vizards', 'properties' and 'tricking' are masks, props (tapers and rattles) and costumes. Step into role as stage designers and sketch some of these resources which will be used in the next fooling of Falstaff.

3 The plots merge

The secret intentions of Page and his wife bring together the Falstaff main plot with the Anne Page sub-plot. Page plans to use the confusion at Herne's Oak to enable Slender to steal away with Anne and marry her. But Mistress Page has her own plan: she thinks Slender is an idiot, and she intends that Anne shall marry Doctor Caius. As you will discover, she too plans to use the midnight mockery of Falstaff as the opportunity for Caius to steal away with Anne. How will the various plots work out? Read on!

jackanapes monkey
taber taper, candle
vizards masks
attirèd dressed
Eton see map on page 164
good will favour
well landed owning much land
best of all affects prefers
Potent powerful
crave her woo her

MISTRESS PAGE The truth being known,
We'll all present ourselves, dis-horn the spirit,
And mock him home to Windsor.
FORD The children must
Be practised well to this, or they'll ne'er do't.
EVANS I will teach the children their behaviours, and I will be like a jackanapes also, to burn the knight with my taber.
FORD That will be excellent. I'll go buy them vizards.
MISTRESS PAGE My Nan shall be the Queen of all the Fairies,
Finely attirèd in a robe of white.
PAGE That silk will I go buy. [*Aside*] And in that time
Shall Master Slender steal my Nan away
And marry her at Eton. [*To Mistress Page and Mistress Ford*]
Go, send to Falstaff straight.
FORD Nay, I'll to him again in name of Brook;
He'll tell me all his purpose. Sure he'll come.
MISTRESS PAGE Fear not you that.

[*To Page, Ford, and Evans*]

Go get us properties
And tricking for our fairies.
EVANS Let us about it. It is admirable pleasures and fery honest knaveries.

[*Exeunt Page, Ford, and Evans*]

MISTRESS PAGE Go, Mistress Ford,
Send quickly to Sir John, to know his mind.

[*Exit Mistress Ford*]

I'll to the Doctor. He hath my good will,
And none but he, to marry with Nan Page.
That Slender, though well landed, is an idiot;
And he my husband best of all affects.
The Doctor is well moneyed, and his friends
Potent at court. He, none but he, shall have her,
Though twenty thousand worthier come to crave her.

[*Exit*]

Simple brings a message from Slender and tells of a fat woman in Falstaff's room. The Host suspects Falstaff is entertaining a prostitute. Falstaff gives Simple a meaningless answer.

---

1 The Host's language (in pairs or groups)

The Host of the Garter uses his familiar exaggerated style as he greets Simple and calls Falstaff. He piles word upon word as he greets Simple, tells him to speak (seven words!), and describes his inn (five nouns). He uses exotic words, more for their elaborate sounds than their meaning, and he repeats phrases for effect.

Take turns to speak all the Host says opposite. Try to express his bluff, cheerful and over-the-top style.

2 An appropriate painting (in pairs or groups)

The Host's description of how Falstaff's room is decorated gives an insight into how many Elizabethan rooms were painted. Falstaff's bedchamber has pictures of the parable of the prodigal son painted on its walls (the story is in the Bible, Luke 15).

a Remind each other of the parable of the prodigal son. In what ways might the parable apply to Falstaff?

b If you go to Stratford-upon-Avon, visit Shakespeare's birthplace, where you will discover some walls are painted in very colourful style, suggesting how the Garter Inn's rooms might be decorated.

3 Saying nothing

Falstaff uses a tautology (words with the same meaning) to make fun of Simple. In lines 28–9, he simply says that the man who cheated ('beguiled') Slender of his chain, cheated ('cozened') him of it.

Make up a few similar sentences using tautology in the same way as Falstaff: sounding meaningful, but saying nothing.

---

boor ill-mannered lout
thick-skin bonehead
Marry by Saint Mary (an oath)
truckle-bed small bed stored under main bed (standing-bed)
Anthropophaginian cannibal
Ephesian drinking partner
Bohemian Tartar barbarian, strange fellow
tarries awaits
Privacy? meeting in private?
wise woman fortune teller
mussel-shell useless and empty-headed

Act 4 Scene 5
The Garter Inn

Enter HOST and SIMPLE

HOST What wouldst thou have, boor? What, thick-skin? Speak, breathe, discuss; brief, short, quick, snap.

SIMPLE Marry, sir, I come to speak with Sir John Falstaff from Master Slender.

HOST There's his chamber, his house, his castle, his standing-bed and truckle-bed. 'Tis painted about with the story of the Prodigal, fresh and new. Go, knock and call. He'll speak like an Anthropophaginian unto thee. Knock, I say.

SIMPLE There's an old woman, a fat woman, gone up into his chamber. I'll be so bold as stay, sir, till she come down. I come to speak with her, indeed.

HOST Ha? A fat woman? The knight may be robbed. I'll call. – Bully knight! Bully Sir John! Speak from thy lungs military. Art thou there? It is thine host, thine Ephesian, calls.

FALSTAFF [*Within*] How now, mine host?

HOST Here's a Bohemian Tartar tarries the coming down of thy fat woman. Let her descend, bully, let her descend. My chambers are honourable. Fie! Privacy? Fie!

[*Enter* FALSTAFF]

FALSTAFF There was, mine host, an old fat woman even now with me, but she's gone.

SIMPLE Pray you, sir, was't not the wise woman of Brentford?

FALSTAFF Ay, marry, was it, mussel-shell. What would you with her?

SIMPLE My master, sir, my Master Slender, sent to her, seeing her go through the streets, to know, sir, whether one Nim, sir, that beguiled him of a chain, had the chain or no.

FALSTAFF I spake with the old woman about it.

SIMPLE And what says she, I pray, sir?

FALSTAFF Marry, she says that the very same man that beguiled Master Slender of his chain cozened him of it.

Falstaff gives Simple another meaningless answer. The Host praises Falstaff's learning, but Falstaff remarks on the hard lesson he learned as the fat woman. Bardolph and Evans warn the Host of robbers.

1 'Paid for my learning': how?

Just what does Falstaff have in mind when he says line 49? And how might he deliver the line on stage to ensure that the audience laughs, knowing full well what he means?

2 The plot against the Host (in small groups)

Shakespeare has been criticised for his portrayal of how Caius and Evans take their revenge on the Host. The episode is briefly enacted in lines 50–73. It seems that the Host has reserved rooms for a German duke who is coming to Court for the Garter ceremony (see pages 148, 158). He has turned away paying guests to do so. He has also loaned horses to some Germans. Now Bardolph, Evans and Caius successively bring him news that the Germans have stolen the horses, have cheated tavern keepers all around Windsor and that the German duke does not exist.

Bardolph tells how the three fraudsters ('cozeners') threw him off his horse into a muddy bog ('slough of mire') and rode off with the horses. He likens them to 'Doctor Faustuses' (in Christopher Marlowe's play *Doctor Faustus* [c.1593], Faustus was granted magical powers by the devil). Evans piles on the agony, reporting that the three Germans have defrauded other innkeepers. When you turn the page you will discover that Doctor Caius adds to the Host's distress, telling that there is no duke of Germany coming to court.

Critics find this revenge sub-plot sketchy and undramatic, but it is all Shakespeare provides, and every new production faces the problem of how to stage lines 50–73 to make convincing drama. How would you do it?

conceal reveal (Simple's malapropism)
like who more bold as brave as the bravest
tidings news
clerkly scholarly, learned
cozenage cheating
varletto varlet, rascal
entertainments hospitality, guests
for good will out of friendship (ironical)
vlouting-stocks laughing-stocks

SIMPLE I would I could have spoken with the woman herself. I had other things to have spoken with her too, from him.

FALSTAFF What are they? Let us know.

HOST Ay, come. Quick!

SIMPLE I may not conceal them, sir.

HOST Conceal them, or thou diest.

SIMPLE Why, sir, they were nothing but about Mistress Anne Page, to know if it were my master's fortune to have her or no.

FALSTAFF 'Tis; 'tis his fortune.

SIMPLE What, sir?

FALSTAFF To have her or no. Go, say the woman told me so.

SIMPLE May I be bold to say so, sir?

FALSTAFF Ay, sir; like who more bold.

SIMPLE I thank your worship. I shall make my master glad with these tidings. [*Exit*]

HOST Thou art clerkly, thou art clerkly, Sir John. Was there a wise woman with thee?

FALSTAFF Ay, that there was, mine host, one that hath taught me more wit than ever I learned before in my life. And I paid nothing for it neither, but was paid for my learning.

[*Enter* BARDOLPH]

BARDOLPH Out, alas, sir, cozenage, mere cozenage!

HOST Where be my horses? Speak well of them, varletto.

BARDOLPH Run away with the cozeners. For so soon as I came beyond Eton, they threw me off from behind one of them in a slough of mire, and set spurs and away, like three German devils, three Doctor Faustuses.

HOST They are gone but to meet the Duke, villain. Do not say they be fled. Germans are honest men.

[*Enter* EVANS]

EVANS Where is mine host?

HOST What is the matter, sir?

EVANS Have a care of your entertainments. There is a friend of mine come to town tells me there is three cozen-Germans that has cozened all the hosts of Readings, of Maidenhead, of Colnbrook, of horses and money. I tell you for good will, look you. You are wise, and full of gibes and vlouting-stocks, and 'tis not convenient you should be cozened. Fare you well. [*Exit*]

Doctor Caius' news panics the Host. He cries for the robbers' arrest. Falstaff reflects on how the court will laugh at how he was tricked. Mistress Quickly brings another invitation from the Wives.

---

1 More bad news for the Host

Caius completes the revenge plot against the Host: there is no duke of Germany ('Jamanie') coming to court. The Host, anguished at the thought of the money he has lost, orders a 'hue and cry', a noisy pursuit of offenders. He leaves with Bardolph, who is part of the conspiracy against him. So just how does Bardolph make his exit? Does he 'Fly, run' as the Host instructs him? Step into role as Bardolph and describe how you will leave the stage.

2 Falstaff's soliloquy (in pairs)

The trick on the Host sets Falstaff thinking about how he too has been duped. He fears that if the Court hears how he was thrown into the Thames, and beaten as the fat woman of Brentford, he would be mocked unmercifully. Talk together about how his two images in lines 77–9 express his sense of humiliation and shame, and about whether you think he is serious as he speaks his final sentence. Then take turns to speak lines 74–81 direct to your partner as audience to express Falstaff's shifting moods.

3 How does she do it? (in pairs)

Mistress Quickly has a very hard task: she must persuade Falstaff to come to the Park at midnight, disguised as Herne the Hunter, to meet the Wives who have so humiliated him earlier. She leaves with Falstaff with that task ahead of her, but the next time they appear (Act 5 Scene 1) she has succeeded. How does she do it? Step into role as Quickly and Falstaff and show how she gets him to take the risk!

---

trot truth
liquor grease
crestfallen as a dried pear downcast and shrivelled
foreswore myself at primero falsely denied cheating in a card game
long enough (to say my prayers)
two parties the Wives
dam wife
bestowed put away
inconstancy changeability
crossed thwarted

[*Enter* CAIUS]

CAIUS Vere is mine host de Jarteer?

HOST Here, Master Doctor, in perplexity and doubtful dilemma.

CAIUS I cannot tell vat is dat; but it is tell-a me dat you make grand preparation for a duke de Jamanie. By my trot, dere is no duke that the court is know to come. I tell you for good will. Adieu. [*Exit*]

HOST [*To Bardolph*] Hue and cry, villain, go! – [*To Falstaff*] Assist me, knight, I am undone! – [*To Bardolph*] Fly, run, hue and cry, villain! I am undone!

[*Exeunt Host and Bardolph*]

FALSTAFF I would all the world might be cozened, for I have been cozened and beaten too. If it should come to the ear of the court how I have been transformed, and how my transformation hath been washed and cudgelled, they would melt me out of my fat drop by drop, and liquor fishermen's boots with me. I warrant they would whip me with their fine wits till I were as crestfallen as a dried pear. I never prospered since I forswore myself at primero. Well, if my wind were but long enough, I would repent.

[*Enter* MISTRESS QUICKLY]

Now, whence come you?

MISTRESS QUICKLY From the two parties, forsooth.

FALSTAFF The devil take one party, and his dam the other, and so they shall be both bestowed. I have suffered more for their sakes, more than the villainous inconstancy of man's disposition is able to bear.

MISTRESS QUICKLY And have not they suffered? Yes, I warrant; speciously one of them. Mistress Ford, good heart, is beaten black and blue, that you cannot see a white spot about her.

FALSTAFF What tell'st thou me of black and blue? I was beaten myself into all the colours of the rainbow; and I was like to be apprehended for the witch of Brentford. But that my admirable dexterity of wit, my counterfeiting the action of an old woman, delivered me, the knave constable had set me i'th'stocks, i'th'common stocks, for a witch.

MISTRESS QUICKLY Sir, let me speak with you in your chamber. You shall hear how things go, and, I warrant, to your content. Here is a letter will say somewhat. Good hearts, what ado here is to bring you together! Sure, one of you does not serve heaven well, that you are so crossed.

FALSTAFF Come up into my chamber. *Exeunt*

The Host is depressed, but agrees to help Fenton, who tells of his and Anne's mutual love. Anne's letter tells of tonight's fooling of Falstaff and of her father's plan that she marry Slender.

'I have a letter from her.' The Host listens as Fenton tells of Anne's letter. It reveals the plan to trick Falstaff, and Anne's scheme to ensure she marries her true love – Master Fenton! You will find activities on Scene 6 on page 136.

give over all stop trying (to help Fenton)
keep your counsel not tell anyone
be her chooser make her own choice of husband
mirth whereof (fooling of Falstaff)
so larded intermixed
my matter things concerning me
manifested achieved, shown
great scene major role to play
image main idea
something rank on foot happening profusely

Act 4 Scene 6
The Garter Inn

Enter FENTON and HOST

HOST Master Fenton, talk not to me. My mind is heavy. I will give over all.

FENTON Yet hear me speak. Assist me in my purpose,
And, as I am a gentleman, I'll give thee
A hundred pound in gold more than your loss.

HOST I will hear you, Master Fenton; and I will, at the least, keep your counsel.

FENTON From time to time I have acquainted you
With the dear love I bear to fair Anne Page,
Who mutually hath answered my affection,
So far forth as herself might be her chooser,
Even to my wish. I have a letter from her,
Of such contents as you will wonder at,
The mirth whereof so larded with my matter
That neither singly can be manifested
Without the show of both. – Fat Falstaff
Hath a great scene. The image of the jest
I'll show you here at large. Hark, good mine host:
Tonight at Herne's Oak, just 'twixt twelve and one,
Must my sweet Nan present the Fairy Queen –
The purpose why is here – in which disguise,
While other jests are something rank on foot,
Her father hath commanded her to slip
Away with Slender, and with him at Eton
Immediately to marry. She hath consented. Now, sir,

Mistress Page has arranged that Doctor Caius spirits Anne away from Herne's Oak and marries her. Anne has agreed to both her mother's and father's plans, but will ensure she marries Fenton!

---

1 Scene 6: activities (in pairs or groups)

Take parts as Fenton and the Host and read the whole scene aloud. Then work together on some of the following activities.

a Write Anne's letter to the Host. It should describe the Wives' plan to humiliate Falstaff and her plan to ensure that she marries Fenton.

b Talk together about why the Host's language is so different from that he has used in other scenes (page 180 can help you).

c Fenton's long exposition must keep the audience's attention throughout. Write a set of director's notes suggesting how the scene could be acted for clarity and dramatic effect. Then take parts and act out the scene.

d A great deal is made of how Anne should be dressed for the ceremonies at Herne's Oak. Her father has arranged that her costume ('habit') as the Fairy Queen shall be white; her mother plans she will be dressed in green. Make a guess as to why colour is so emphasised here. Check your guess as you read Act 5.

e Shakespeare chooses to have Fenton report Anne's agreement to both her father's and her mother's plan, rather than to dramatise it. Improvise the two missing scenes in which the daughter deceives both parents.

f Identify the three lines (on page 135) where Shakespeare as a dramatist seems to be saying 'This is where the Falstaff main plot and the Anne Page sub-plot intertwine.'

---

ever strong against always opposing
other sports are tasking of their minds people are busy with other things
dean'ry dean's house
pendent flaring hanging and flowing
spies his vantage ripe sees his best opportunity
husband your device manage your plan carefully
present recompense immediate reward

Her mother, ever strong against that match
And firm for Doctor Caius, hath appointed
That he shall likewise shuffle her away,
While other sports are tasking of their minds,
And at the dean'ry, where a priest attends,
Straight marry her. To this her mother's plot
She, seemingly obedient, likewise hath
Made promise to the Doctor. Now thus it rests:
Her father means she shall be all in white,
And in that habit, when Slender sees his time
To take her by the hand and bid her go,
She shall go with him. Her mother hath intended,
The better to denote her to the Doctor –
For they must all be masked and vizarded –
That quaint in green she shall be loose enrobed,
With ribbons pendent flaring 'bout her head;
And when the Doctor spies his vantage ripe,
To pinch her by the hand, and, on that token,
The maid hath given consent to go with him.

HOST Which means she to deceive, father or mother?

FENTON Both, my good host, to go along with me.
And here it rests, that you'll procure the vicar
To stay for me at church 'twixt twelve and one,
And, in the lawful name of marrying,
To give our hearts united ceremony.

HOST Well, husband your device. I'll to the vicar.
Bring you the maid, you shall not lack a priest.

FENTON So shall I evermore be bound to thee;
Besides, I'll make a present recompense.

Exeunt

Looking back at Act 4

Activities for groups or individuals

In this staging of Scene 1, Mistress Quickly covers William's ears so that he cannot hear the bad language she thinks Evans' Latin lesson expresses. Turn back to Scene 1 and suggest at which line this photograph was taken.

1 No problem because it's a comedy?

In Scene 2, Falstaff gets a battering from Ford who thinks he is beating the fat woman of Brentford. In Scene 5, Mistress Quickly reports (falsely) that Ford has beaten Mistress Ford 'black and blue'. No one in the play makes any comment on this violence towards women. What is your view? Is there any point in discussing the beatings seriously?

2 Shakespeare explains

In Act 4, the Falstaff plot and the Anne Page sub-plot begin to interweave. Imagine you are Shakespeare giving a talk to his acting company as they prepare to put on the play. Explain just how you have arranged for the two strands of the play to come together.

3 Appearance and reality

Appearance and reality is a common theme of every Shakespeare play: things are not as they seem. Briefly identify how the theme occurs in each of the six scenes in Act 4.

4 Is she a snob?

Why does Mistress Page prefer Caius as a husband for Anne? Identify her reasons in Scene 4, lines 80–6 and say how they affect your view of her.

5 'This tale of Herne the Hunter'

Remind yourself of the story Mistress Page tells in Scene 4, lines 25–35. Then step into role as Shakespeare, read the following tale, and rewrite it as additional lines in blank verse for Mistress Page to speak.

> The legend goes that in Windsor Great Park, Herne, a hunter, had saved a king from being killed by throwing himself upon a stag and suffering terrible injuries. A wizard appeared and told the king the only way to save Herne was to cut off the stag's antlers and tie them to Herne's head. Herne revived and became the king's chief forester. His hunting skills were envied by the other foresters, and they planned to kill him. They met at night in Windsor Park where a mysterious rider offered them help in return for 'payment' later. Herne's hunting skills failed him and the king dismissed him. That night a terrible storm raged over Windsor, and the next day Herne's body was found hanging from a great oak tree in the Park.
>
> In the weeks that followed, deer went missing, and there were tales of a ghostly midnight rider who looked like Herne with huge antlers on his forehead. The foresters who had conspired against Herne met again at the oak where the mysterious stranger appeared and revealed himself as the devil. He condemned them to hunt each night with the ghostly Herne, killing the king's deer. They did so, but finally, utterly exhausted, confessed to the king who had them all hanged from Herne's Oak, mocked by the devil's laughter. Ever since, the terrifying horned figure of Herne leading his ghostly band of huntsmen has been seen galloping at midnight through Windsor Park.

Falstaff promises he will keep the appointment at Herne's Oak. He tells Brook (Ford) that he visited Mistress Ford again, but Ford thrashed him soundly. He plans revenge on Ford tonight.

1 Third time lucky?

Falstaff has twice suffered grievously for attempting to seduce Mistress Ford. He hopes to succeed in his third attempt, and reflects on the Elizabethan belief that it was fortunate to be born, die or attempt anything on an odd numbered day. A well-known proverb of the time was 'the third time pays for all'. You will soon discover whether Falstaff's hope is realised.

2 Shakespeare sets puzzles (in small groups)

There are four puzzling features of Scene 1:

Line 5 – 'a chain': the chain is never mentioned again.

Line 11 – 'yesterday': Falstaff visited Mistress Ford that morning.

Lines 18-19 – 'I fear not … shuttle': see foot of page. Is he saying he does not fear a giant's spear because life passes speedily?

The fourth puzzle is that there is no soliloquy for Ford. On previous visits to Falstaff, Ford was given a soliloquy at the end of the scene in which he revealed his feelings. This time he says nothing. Write a short soliloquy for him. Remember, this time he knows what his wife really does intend for Falstaff!

3 Images of childhood (in small groups)

Falstaff says the last time he was beaten was as a child. He provides a vivid image of childhood as a time when he 'plucked geese, played truant and whipped top'. Make up a few of your own images of childhood using Falstaff's as a model.

I'll hold I'll keep my word
divinity godlike power
time wears time passes
mince walk in an affected manner (because you've achieved your purpose)
governed frenzy ruled madness
Goliath with a weaver's beam In the Bible, the shaft of Goliath's spear 'was like a weaver's beam' (1 Samuel 17.7)
shuttle another biblical quotation: 'my days pass more speedily than a weaver's shuttle' (Book of Job 7.6)

Act 5 Scene 1
The Garter Inn

Enter FALSTAFF and MISTRESS QUICKLY

FALSTAFF Prithee, no more prattling; go. I'll hold. This is the third time; I hope good luck lies in odd numbers. Away, go! They say there is divinity in odd numbers, either in nativity, chance, or death. Away!

MISTRESS QUICKLY I'll provide you a chain, and I'll do what I can to get you a pair of horns.

FALSTAFF Away, I say; time wears. Hold up your head, and mince.

[*Exit Mistress Quickly*]

[*Enter* FORD *disguised as Brook*]

How now, Master Brook! Master Brook, the matter will be known tonight or never. Be you in the Park about midnight, at Herne's Oak, and you shall see wonders.

FORD Went you not to her yesterday, sir, as you told me you had appointed?

FALSTAFF I went to her, Master Brook, as you see, like a poor old man, but I came from her, Master Brook, like a poor old woman. That same knave Ford, her husband, hath the finest mad devil of jealousy in him, Master Brook, that ever governed frenzy. I will tell you he beat me grievously, in the shape of a woman; for in the shape of man, Master Brook, I fear not Goliath with a weaver's beam, because I know also life is a shuttle. I am in haste. Go along with me. I'll tell you all, Master Brook. Since I plucked geese, played truant, and whipped top, I knew not what 'twas to be beaten till lately. Follow me. I'll tell you strange things of this knave Ford, on whom tonight I will be revenged, and I will deliver his wife into your hand. Follow. Strange things in hand, Master Brook! Follow.

Exeunt

Slender prepares to steal away with Anne during the humiliation of Falstaff. He and the female in white will exchange passwords. Mistress Page plans for Caius to run off with Anne.

---

1 **Preparations!** (in groups of three)

Three short scenes (2, 3 and 4) show preparations of two very different kinds. Slender and Caius get ready to steal away with Anne Page and marry her, and arrangements are made for the sport of mocking Falstaff. To gain a first understanding of what is going on, take parts and read through all three scenes, then work on some of the activities below and on page 144.

a *An interruption.* Slender interrupts Page at line 2. Make your suggestions as to what Page was about to say.

b *Entrances and exits.* In the modern theatre, it is conventional for scenes to follow each other in swift succession. One scene 'flows into' the next. In contrast, in Victorian times there were often long pauses between scenes, sometimes involving complex changes of scenery. In Shakespeare's time, on the open Globe stage, there would have been the minimum of scenery, and, as today, as one scene ended, the next began.

But just how does one set of actors get off stage, and how does the next group come on? One production had the Wives almost bump into Page, and bundling Caius away to avoid being seen. Work out how you would stage the entrances and exits for Scenes 2, 3 and 4 in ways that give the audience a sense of continuing action building towards a dramatic climax.

c *Marital relations.* What do lines 7–9 in Scene 3 suggest about the relationship of Page and Mistress Page? Who does Mistress Page have in mind when she talks of 'heartbreak'?

---

couch i'th'Castle ditch lie hidden in Windsor Castle's ditch
son son-in-law
forsooth truly
nay-word password
'mum', 'budget' the two words combine as 'mumbudget' (silence)
become it suit the dark night
dispatch it quickly marry her instantly
chiding scolding

Act 5 Scene 2
Windsor: a street

Enter PAGE, SHALLOW, and SLENDER

PAGE Come, come, we'll couch i'th'Castle ditch till we see the light of our fairies. Remember, son Slender, my –

SLENDER Ay, forsooth, I have spoke with her, and we have a nay-word how to know one another. I come to her in white and cry 'mum'; she cries 'budget'; and by that we know one another.

SHALLOW That's good too. But what needs either your 'mum' or her 'budget'? The white will decipher her well enough. – It hath struck ten o'clock.

PAGE The night is dark. Light and spirits will become it well: Heaven prosper our sport! No man means evil but the devil, and we shall know him by his horns. Let's away. Follow me.

Exeunt

Act 5 Scene 3
Master Page's house

Enter MISTRESS PAGE, MISTRESS FORD, and CAIUS

MISTRESS PAGE Master Doctor, my daughter is in green. When you see your time, take her by the hand, away with her to the deanery, and dispatch it quickly. Go before into the Park. We two must go together.

CAIUS I know vat I have to do. Adieu.

MISTRESS PAGE Fare you well, sir.

[*Exit Caius*]

My husband will not rejoice so much at the abuse of Falstaff as he will chafe at the Doctor's marrying my daughter. But 'tis no matter. Better a little chiding than a great deal of heartbreak.

MISTRESS FORD Where is Nan now, and her troop of fairies, and the Welsh devil Hugh?

MISTRESS PAGE They are all couched in a pit hard by Herne's Oak, with obscured lights, which, at the very instant of Falstaff's and our meeting, they will at once display to the night.

The Wives relish the prospect of Falstaff's approaching humiliation. Evans prepares his fairy band for action. Falstaff calls on the lustful gods to help him. He reflects on the transformations effected by love.

---

1 **The biter bit** (in pairs)

The Wives look forward to Falstaff receiving his come-uppance, and Mistress Page speaks a couplet that justifies their punishment of the fat knight (lines 19–20). Make up a couplet in similar style that expresses approximately the same meaning.

2 **Fairy costumes** (in pairs)

Evans is disguised as a satyr, a woodland god with the ears, tail and legs of a goat (and also renowned for its sexual appetite). But how might the fairies be dressed? Sketch some ideas for their costumes.

3 **Amorous adventures** (in pairs)

Falstaff's soliloquy uses imagery from classical mythology. Jove, king of the gods, disguised himself as a bull. He tempted Europa to climb on his back, then swam off with her to ravish her. Jupiter (another name for Jove) disguised himself as a swan in order to have sex with Leda.

Falstaff plays with the idea that love turns man into a beast. Prompted by the thought that the gods themselves become animals or birds to indulge their lust, he imagines himself as the fattest stag in Windsor forest. But he seems nervous of the sexual adventures he imagines are to come. After the hot-blooded exploits of Jove, he hopes for a cool mating time so that he does not lose his fat. The heat of mating was thought to be the cause of stags growing thin in rutting time, resulting in them urinating their fat ('tallow') away.

Speak Falstaff's soliloquy to express his feelings about what he thinks is about to happen.

---

cannot choose but amaze is bound to frighten
lewdsters lechers, sex maniacs
Trib trip
complexion appearance
hot backs sexual urges
rut-time mating time
piss my tallow urinate my fat away

MISTRESS FORD That cannot choose but amaze him.

MISTRESS PAGE If he be not amazed, he will be mocked. If he be amazed, he will every way be mocked.

MISTRESS FORD We'll betray him finely.

MISTRESS PAGE Against such lewdsters and their lechery,
Those that betray them do no treachery.

MISTRESS FORD The hour draws on. To the Oak, to the Oak!

Exeunt

Act 5 Scene 4
Near Herne's Oak

Enter EVANS dressed like a satyr, and boys dressed like fairies

EVANS Trib, trib, fairies! Come, and remember your parts. Be pold, I pray you. Follow me into the pit, and when I give the watch-'ords, do as I pid you. Come, come; trib, trib!

Exeunt

Act 5 Scene 5
Herne's Oak

Enter FALSTAFF disguised as Herne with a buck's head upon him

FALSTAFF The Windsor bell hath struck twelve; the minute draws on. Now, the hot-blooded gods assist me! Remember, Jove, thou wast a bull for thy Europa. Love set on thy horns. O powerful love, that in some respects makes a beast a man, in some other a man a beast! You were also, Jupiter, a swan for the love of Leda. O omnipotent love, how near the god drew to the complexion of a goose! A fault done first in the form of a beast: O Jove, a beastly fault! And then another fault in the semblance of a fowl: think on't, Jove, a foul fault! When gods have hot backs, what shall poor men do? For me, I am here a Windsor stag, and the fattest, I think, i'th'forest. Send me a cool rut-time, Jove, or who can blame me to piss my tallow? Who comes here? My doe?

Falstaff envisages an erotic encounter with the Wives. He thinks his suffering is about to be sexually rewarded. But the entry of Evans and the fairies looks set to dash his hopes.

---

1 **At last! (I)** (in pairs)

Lines 13–17 bristle with erotic anticipation. A knowledge of what Elizabethans would have understood by the lines can help your own understanding of how passion fills Falstaff's being:

'scut': short tail, and female genitals.

'potatoes': yams, sweet potatoes, thought to be aphrodisiacs.

'kissing-comfits': perfumed sugar-plums, to sweeten a lover's breath.

'eryngoes': candied sea holly, thought to be an aphrodisiac.

'provocation': erotic stimulation.

So what might Falstaff do as he says 'I will shelter me here'?

2 **At last! (II)** (in pairs)

Learning that Mistress Page has also come along, Falstaff thinks he will enjoy both wives, and in lines 19–23 proposes they divide him between them. He thinks that at last Cupid is making amends for all the humiliation he has suffered. So what might he do as he exclaims 'welcome!'?

3 **The masque begins** (in pairs)

Falstaff's hopes are shattered as the Wives put their plan into action. With the entry of Evans and the others, the scene becomes a type of masque: an elaborate spectacle in which fantastically costumed participants speak in formal verse. You will find activities on page 148, but for the moment talk about whether you think the 'radiant Queen' who hates dirtiness and immorality (line 39) refers to Queen Elizabeth I, the Queen of the Fairies, or both.

---

bribed buck stolen stag
fellow of this walk keeper of this part of the park
woodman hunter, wild man
orphan (fairies have no parents)
fixèd destiny unchangeable duties
office, quality duties
Hobgoblin Puck, Robin Goodfellow, the fairies' town cryer
oyes oyez, hear ye
Cricket a fairy's name
unraked gone cold

[*Enter* MISTRESS FORD *and* MISTRESS PAGE]

MISTRESS FORD Sir John! Art thou there, my deer, my male deer?

FALSTAFF My doe with the black scut! Let the sky rain potatoes, let it thunder to the tune of 'Greensleeves', hail kissing-comfits, and snow eryngoes; let there come a tempest of provocation, I will shelter me here.

[*He embraces her*]

MISTRESS FORD Mistress Page is come with me, sweetheart.

FALSTAFF Divide me like a bribed buck, each a haunch. I will keep my sides to myself, my shoulders for the fellow of this walk, and my horns I bequeath your husbands. Am I a woodman, ha? Speak I like Herne the Hunter? Why, now is Cupid a child of conscience: he makes restitution. As I am a true spirit, welcome!

[*A noise of horns within*]

MISTRESS PAGE Alas, what noise?

MISTRESS FORD Heaven forgive our sins!

FALSTAFF What should this be?

MISTRESS FORD *and* MISTRESS PAGE Away, away!

[*They run off*]

FALSTAFF I think the devil will not have me damned, lest the oil that's in me should set hell on fire. He would never else cross me thus.

Enter [EVANS *like a satyr with a lighted taper in his hand, and boys dressed like*] *fairies* [*with lighted tapers on their heads; the boy who played the part of Mistress Quickly disguised as the* QUEEN OF FAIRIES, *the actor who played the part of Pistol disguised as* HOBGOBLIN, *and* ANNE PAGE *disguised as a fairy*]

QUEEN OF FAIRIES Fairies black, grey, green, and white,
You moonshine revellers, and shades of night,
You orphan heirs of fixèd destiny,
Attend your office and your quality.
Crier Hobgoblin, make the fairy oyes.

HOBGOBLIN Elves, list your names; silence, you airy toys.
Cricket, to Windsor chimneys shalt thou leap.
Where fires thou find'st unraked and hearths unswept,
There pinch the maids as blue as bilberry:
Our radiant Queen hates sluts and sluttery.

Evans orders the reward of dutiful Christians and the punishment of sinners. The Queen of the Fairies orders preparations to be made for the Garter ceremony. A dance is prepared – but Falstaff is discovered!

---

1 Emphasise the rhymes? (in small groups)

The actors playing the fairies use rhyming couplets. Speak lines 30–95 around the group, with one person speaking the first two lines, the second the next two lines, and so on. Emphasise the rhymes as you speak. Afterwards, talk together about whether you think actors should emphasise the rhymes in performance.

2 The Garter ceremony (in pairs)

Some critics believe that lines 49–66 were written specially to celebrate the ceremony of installing Knights of the Garter in St George's Chapel in Windsor Castle. You can find out more about this on page 158, but for now imagine you are the Queen of the Fairies instructing an extremely stupid bunch of elves and fairies who need to see physical actions to understand their orders. Take turns to speak the lines, accompanying your words with actions. Use the following explanations and those at the foot of the page to help you.

'chairs of order': stalls (seats) of the Knights of the Garter.

'instalment': stall (seat).

'coat': coat of arms.

'crest': plume on helmet of knight.

'blazon': banner bearing coat of arms.

'*Honi soit qui mal y pense*': shame to him who evil thinks (the motto of the Garter). King Edward III, who founded the Order of the Garter, is said to have picked up the fallen garter of the Countess of Salisbury. He fixed it to his own knee saying these words to put down any sniggering watchers.

---

couch lie hidden
Raise up … fantasy give her sweet dreams
oafs elves
perpetual doom day of judgement
state, state condition, dignity
owner Queen Elizabeth I
scour scrub, clean
compass circle
expressure image, picture
charactery writing
measure dance
man of middle earth mortal (earth was imagined to be between heaven and hell)

FALSTAFF [*Aside*] They are fairies; he that speaks to them shall die.
I'll wink and couch; no man their works must eye.

[*He lies down and hides his face*]

EVANS Where's Bead? Go you, and where you find a maid
That ere she sleep has thrice her prayers said,
Raise up the organs of her fantasy;
Sleep she as sound as careless infancy.
But those as sleep and think not on their sins,
Pinch them, arms, legs, backs, shoulders, sides, and shins.
QUEEN OF FAIRIES About, about!
Search Windsor Castle, elves, within and out.
Strew good luck, oafs, on every sacred room,
That it may stand till the perpetual doom
In state as wholesome as in state 'tis fit,
Worthy the owner and the owner it.
The several chairs of order look you scour
With juice of balm and every precious flower.
Each fair instalment, coat, and several crest,
With loyal blazon, evermore be blest!
And nightly meadow-fairies, look you sing,
Like to the Garter's compass, in a ring.
Th'expressure that it bears, green let it be,
More fertile-fresh than all the field to see;
And *Honi soit qui mal y pense* write
In em'rald tufts, flowers purple, blue, and white,
Like sapphire, pearl, and rich embroidery,
Buckled below fair knighthood's bending knee.
Fairies use flowers for their charactery.
Away, disperse! – But till 'tis one o'clock,
Our dance of custom round about the oak
Of Herne the Hunter let us not forget.
EVANS Pray you, lock hand in hand; yourselves in order set;
And twenty glow-worms shall our lanterns be,
To guide our measure round about the tree. –
But stay! I smell a man of middle earth!
FALSTAFF [*Aside*] Heavens defend me from that Welsh fairy, lest he transform me to a piece of cheese!

Evans singes Falstaff's finger. His pained reaction makes the fairies taunt, pinch and scorch him. Fenton, unlike Caius and Slender, makes off with the real Anne Page. Page and his wife mock Falstaff.

'Fie on lust and luxury!' Trial by the ordeal of fire was thought to test innocence. Falstaff's pained reaction is taken as proof of his guilt, and the fairies chant their condemnation of his vices.

1 **Perform the stage directions** (in large groups)

Caius, Slender and Fenton, under cover of the fairies' torment of Falstaff, each make their escape with the fairy they believe to be Anne Page. But only Fenton has the real Anne! Work out your own performance of lines 70–95. Make sure your audience can see and understand just what is happening in the stage direction at line 95.

o'erlooked bewitched, gazed on by the evil eye
trial-fire testing fire, ordeal by fire
chaste honest, pure
trip dance
luxury lechery
bloody fire consuming passion
mutually all together
hold up the jest no higher prolong the joke no further
yokes antlers, cuckold's horns
Become suit, fit

HOBGOBLIN [*To Falstaff*]
Vile worm, thou wast o'erlooked even in thy birth.
QUEEN OF FAIRIES [*To Evans*] With trial-fire touch me his finger-end.
If he be chaste, the flame will back descend
And turn him to no pain; but if he start,
It is the flesh of a corrupted heart.
HOBGOBLIN A trial, come!
EVANS Come, will this wood take fire?

[*Evans puts the taper to Falstaff's finger, and he starts*]

FALSTAFF O, O, O!
QUEEN OF FAIRIES Corrupt, corrupt, and tainted in desire!
About him, fairies, sing a scornful rhyme,
And, as you trip, still pinch him to your time.

[*Fairies dance around Falstaff, pinching and burning him*]

FAIRIES [*Sing*] Fie on sinful fantasy!
Fie on lust and luxury!
Lust is but a bloody fire,
Kindled with unchaste desire
Fed in heart, whose flames aspire,
As thoughts do blow them, higher and higher.
Pinch him, fairies, mutually;
Pinch him for his villainy.
Pinch him, and burn him, and turn him about,
Till candles and starlight and moonshine be out.

[*During the song, enter* CAIUS *at one door and steals away a Fairy in green; enter* SLENDER *at another door and steals away the Queen of Fairies in white; enter* FENTON *and steals away Anne Page. After the song a noise of hunting horns within. The Fairies run away from Falstaff but do not exit. Falstaff pulls off his buck's head, and rises.*]

[*Enter* PAGE *and* MISTRESS PAGE, *and* FORD *and* MISTRESS FORD]

PAGE Nay, do not fly; I think we have watched you now.
Will none but Herne the Hunter serve your turn?
MISTRESS PAGE I pray you, come, hold up the jest no higher. –
Now, good Sir John, how like you Windsor wives?

[*Pointing to the horns*]

See you these, husband? Do not these fair yokes
Become the forest better than the town?

Ford mocks Falstaff, who admits his foolishness in being deceived. Evans advises Falstaff to abandon lust, and Ford to abandon jealousy. Falstaff criticises Evans' pronunciation. Mistress Page, Ford and Page ridicule Falstaff.

---

1 Mocking Falstaff (I) (in pairs)

Ford's lines 102–6 are highly patterned and rhythmical as he keeps repeating 'Master Brook' in mocking imitation of Falstaff's repetition of the name in earlier scenes. Try speaking the lines first in a sing-song, jeering way with heavy ironic emphasis on each 'Master Brook'. Then experiment with different styles of delivery.

2 Recognition – and recovery? (in pairs)

Falstaff has four speeches opposite. He realises he has been fooled, and blames himself for falling for such a crude trick ('grossness of the foppery'). But he rallies, and criticises Evans' Welsh accent that 'makes fritters of English'. One person speaks all he says, a sentence at a time. After each sentence the others suggest answers to each of the following questions:

a Does he speak to himself? The audience? A character? or …?

b How might he deliver each line to increase comic effect?

3 Mocking Falstaff (II) (in pairs)

Mistress Page asks how Falstaff could ever have thought that, even if the Wives wished to sin, they would give themselves to him (lines 132–5): 'made you our delight?' Her contemptuous remark unleashes a brief stream of abuse towards Falstaff. Consider each insult in lines 136–44 and talk together about what each means, and whether you think the speaker delivers it with venom, or good humour, or dismissively, or in some other way.

---

extant evident (the horns)
received belief firm conviction
Jack-a-Lent see page 80
wants matter lacks substance
gross o'erreaching crude trickery
coxcomb of frieze fool's cap of coarse woollen cloth
late-walking seeking sex at night
hodge-pudding pudding of mixed ingredients
Satan, Job, wife in the Bible, Satan's slanders persuaded God to afflict Job with poverty. Job's wife tempted him to curse God

FORD Now, sir, who's a cuckold now? Master Brook, Falstaff's a knave, a cuckoldy knave. Here are his horns, Master Brook. And, Master Brook, he hath enjoyed nothing of Ford's but his buck-basket, his cudgel, and twenty pounds of money, which must be paid to Master Brook. His horses are arrested for it, Master Brook.

MISTRESS FORD Sir John, we have had ill luck; we could never meet. I will never take you for my love again, but I will always count you my deer.

FALSTAFF I do begin to perceive that I am made an ass.

FORD Ay, and an ox too. Both the proofs are extant.

FALSTAFF And these are not fairies. I was three or four times in the thought they were not fairies; and yet the guiltiness of my mind, the sudden surprise of my powers, drove the grossness of the foppery into a received belief, in despite of the teeth of all rhyme and reason, that they were fairies. See now how wit may be made a Jack-a-Lent when 'tis upon ill employment!

EVANS [*Discarding his disguise*] Sir John Falstaff, serve Got, and leave your desires, and fairies will not pinse you.

FORD Well said, fairy Hugh.

EVANS And leave you your jealousies too, I pray you.

FORD I will never mistrust my wife again till thou art able to woo her in good English.

FALSTAFF Have I laid my brain in the sun and dried it, that it wants matter to prevent so gross o'erreaching as this? Am I ridden with a Welsh goat too? Shall I have a coxcomb of frieze? 'Tis time I were choked with a piece of toasted cheese.

EVANS Seese is not good to give putter. Your belly is all putter.

FALSTAFF 'Seese' and 'putter'? Have I lived to stand at the taunt of one that makes fritters of English? This is enough to be the decay of lust and late-walking through the realm.

MISTRESS PAGE Why, Sir John, do you think, though we would have thrust virtue out of our hearts by the head and shoulders, and have given ourselves without scruple to hell, that ever the devil could have made you our delight?

FORD What, a hodge-pudding? A bag of flax?

MISTRESS PAGE A puffed man?

PAGE Old, cold, withered, and of intolerable entrails?

FORD And one that is as slanderous as Satan?

PAGE And as poor as Job?

FORD And as wicked as his wife?

Falstaff gives up, admitting he has been humbled. Ford jeers about the money Falstaff must repay, but Page offers reconciliation. Slender is devastated to find he almost married a postmaster's boy!

---

1 In the dumps? (in pairs)

Falstaff acknowledges that he is thoroughly beaten. His six short sentences opposite are all admissions that he is now completely at the mercy of the mockery of the Windsor citizens. But in performance the actor playing Falstaff decides whether to show the fat knight is utterly serious, feeling genuinely depressed and defeated, or whether he is trying to laugh off his humiliation, or whether he is play-acting, pretending submission, but not meaning a word of what he says.

What do you think? Write notes to guide Falstaff through his delivery of lines 145–7.

2 Forgiveness – with an ulterior motive!

After all Falstaff's wrongdoings and humiliations, Page offers friendship. He invites Falstaff to drink at his house tonight. But Page's offer is also intended as a chance to mock his wife, because he thinks his own preferred son-in-law, Slender, has married Anne. What kind of laughter does Page have in mind when he says he wants Falstaff to 'laugh at my wife'?

3 Act it out! (in groups of three)

Page's cheerfulness is quickly dashed as Slender enters complaining that he took away the wrong Anne Page to church. He did everything as planned, but ended up with a postmaster's boy! Lines 157–75 can make an hilarious episode in performance. Take parts as Page, Slender and a director. Prepare your own performance of the episode and perform it to the class.

---

metheglins spiced Welsh mead
starings bravado, swaggerings
pribbles and prabbles bickering and squabbling
theme subject matter (for laughter)
start advantage
is a plummet o'er me sounds my depths (got to the bottom of me)
cozened cheated
pander pimp
eat a posset share a hot drink
lubberly clumsy, loutish
swinged thrashed

EVANS And given to fornications, and to taverns, and sack, and wine, and metheglins, and to drinkings, and swearings and starings, pribbles and prabbles?

FALSTAFF Well, I am your theme. You have the start of me. I am dejected. I am not able to answer the Welsh flannel. Ignorance itself is a plummet o'er me. Use me as you will.

FORD Marry, sir, we'll bring you to Windsor, to one Master Brook, that you have cozened of money, to whom you should have been a pander. Over and above that you have suffered, I think to repay that money will be a biting affliction.

PAGE Yet be cheerful, knight. Thou shalt eat a posset tonight at my house, where I will desire thee to laugh at my wife that now laughs at thee. Tell her Master Slender hath married her daughter.

MISTRESS PAGE [*Aside*] Doctors doubt that. If Anne Page be my daughter, she is, by this, Doctor Caius' wife.

[*Enter* SLENDER]

SLENDER Whoa, ho, ho, father Page!

PAGE Son, how now! How now, son! Have you dispatched?

SLENDER Dispatched? I'll make the best in Gloucestershire know on't. Would I were hanged, la, else!

PAGE Of what, son?

SLENDER I came yonder at Eton to marry Mistress Anne Page, and she's a great lubberly boy. If it had not been i'th'church, I would have swinged him, or he should have swinged me. If I did not think it had been Anne Page, would I might never stir! And 'tis a postmaster's boy!

PAGE Upon my life, then, you took the wrong.

SLENDER What need you tell me that? I think so, when I took a boy for a girl. If I had been married to him, for all he was in woman's apparel, I would not have had him.

PAGE Why, this is your own folly. Did not I tell you how you should know my daughter by her garments?

SLENDER I went to her in white, and cried 'mum', and she cried 'budget', as Anne and I had appointed. And yet it was not Anne, but a postmaster's boy. [*Exit*]

MISTRESS PAGE Good George, be not angry. I knew of your purpose, turned my daughter into green, and indeed she is now with the Doctor at the deanery, and there married.

[*Enter* CAIUS]

Caius is affronted: he too nearly married a boy! Fenton explains: he and Anne are married, unhappiness is avoided. The Pages welcome Fenton as a son-in-law, and Falstaff is invited to tonight's party.

---

1 Follow that! (in pairs)

In comparison with Slender's disclosure that he nearly married a boy, Doctor Caius has only four lines with which to set the audience laughing. Slender's complaint usually provokes a great deal of audience laughter – so how might Caius make sure his few lines make them laugh even more?

2 Falstaff gains some comfort (in pairs)

Falstaff uses a hunting metaphor to say he is cheered that although Page and his wife took up a 'stand' against him (a position from which huntsmen stood to shoot arrows), both have both failed ('your arrow hath glanced') in their marriage plans for Anne. He has another jibe at them in line 208, but it is not quite clear how his remark fits the situation. Make your own suggestion of what he might mean.

3 Stage the reconciliation (in groups of six)

Just how do Page and Mistress Page come to accept Fenton as a son-in-law? How do they react through Fenton's speech and to Ford's claim that love, not money, is important in marriage? Take parts and speak lines 185–210, then talk together about how 'your' character behaves throughout the episode. Are Page and Mistress Page entirely sincere in their acceptance?

4 Exeunt – and final image (in pairs)

How does everyone leave the stage (*Exeunt*)? Step into role as director and write notes on how you will stage the closing moments. Also specify the final 'stage picture' the audience will see in your production of the play. Give your reasons for that final image.

---

paysan peasant, yokel
no proportion held in love no proper loving relationship
contracted engaged, betrothed
so sure firmly united in marriage
evitate avoid
guide the state rule
eschewed avoided
night-dogs out-of-control dogs (?)
muse grumble

CAIUS Vere is Mistress Page? By gar, I am cozened. I ha' married *un garçon*, a boy; *un paysan*, by gar, a boy. It is not Anne Page. By gar, I am cozened.

MISTRESS PAGE Why? Did you take her in green?

CAIUS Ay, by gar, and 'tis a boy. By gar, I'll raise all Windsor. [*Exit*]

FORD This is strange. Who hath got the right Anne?

[*Enter* FENTON *and* ANNE PAGE]

PAGE My heart misgives me. Here comes Master Fenton.
How now, Master Fenton!

ANNE Pardon, good father. Good my mother, pardon.

PAGE Now, mistress, how chance you went not with Master Slender?

MISTRESS PAGE Why went you not with Master Doctor, maid?

FENTON You do amaze her. Hear the truth of it.
You would have married her most shamefully
Where there was no proportion held in love.
The truth is, she and I, long since contracted,
Are now so sure that nothing can dissolve us.
Th'offence is holy that she hath committed,
And this deceit loses the name of craft,
Of disobedience, or unduteous title,
Since therein she doth evitate and shun
A thousand irreligious cursèd hours
Which forcèd marriage would have brought upon her.

FORD Stand not amazed. Here is no remedy.
In love the heavens themselves do guide the state.
Money buys lands, and wives are sold by fate.

FALSTAFF I am glad, though you have ta'en a special stand to strike at me, that your arrow hath glanced.

PAGE Well, what remedy? Fenton, heaven give thee joy!
What cannot be eschewed must be embraced.

FALSTAFF When night-dogs run, all sorts of deer are chased.

MISTRESS PAGE Well, I will muse no further. – Master Fenton
Heaven give you many, many merry days! –
Good husband, let us every one go home,
And laugh this sport o'er by a country fire,
Sir John and all.

FORD Let it be so, Sir John.
To Master Brook you yet shall hold your word,
For he tonight shall lie with Mistress Ford.

Exeunt

Looking back at the play

Activities for groups or individuals

1 The Order of the Garter

In the play's final scene, the Queen of the Fairies orders her followers to prepare for the ceremony of installing new Knights of the Order of the Garter. In Shakespeare's time, the installation of newly elected Knights of the Garter was accompanied by lavish celebrations: feasting, plays and elaborate entertainments. Some critics believe that the play was first performed at the Garter celebrations on 23 April 1597 when the patron of Shakespeare's acting company, Lord Hunsdon the Lord Chamberlain, was installed as a Knight of the Garter. It is thought that Lord Hunsdon commissioned Shakespeare to write the play as a contribution to the entertainments – but gave him very short notice. At the same ceremony, the Duke of Wurtemberg was also elected to the Order (but did not attend in person). Perhaps Shakespeare inserted the episode of the Germans who steal the Host's horses and the 'duke of Jamanie' who does not turn up, in order to amuse the Garter audience.

- Imagine you were present at the Garter ceremony in 1597. Write your account of what you saw – including the play!

2 Who changes?

In all of Shakespeare's plays, certain characters change as a result of what they experience in the play. Turn to the List of characters on page 1. Consider each character in turn and say whether, and in what way, they are different at the end of the play from at the beginning.

3 Windsor or Stratford?

Step into role as Shakespeare. Give your reasons for setting the play in Windsor, rather than in Stratford-upon-Avon, the country town you know best.

4 Professor Profundo explains

Step into role as Professor Profundo and give your learned lecture on the play which interprets Falstaff's humiliation as the sacrifice of a fertility god which signifies the defeat of winter.

'I came yonder at Eton to marry Mistress Anne Page, and she's a great lubberly boy.' Slender is aghast that he nearly married the postmaster's boy! Do characters get what they deserve? Give your reply for Falstaff, Slender and Caius. Also say whether you feel sympathy for any of these three characters at the end of the play.

5 Five years on

Step into role as either Anne Page or Master Fenton and tell what has happened in Windsor during the five years since the play's end.

6 Stage props

Make a list of the props (stage properties) any production of the play needs. Illustrate your list with designs of some props.

What is the play about?

There are all kinds of ways of thinking about *The Merry Wives of Windsor*. For example, you could see it as a play of intrigue, plot and counter-plot, in which Falstaff gets his come-uppance as 'the biter bit'. It has also been described as a farce, a jolly romp, and as a comic morality play in which values are tested and virtue triumphs over vice. It is a play about love, greed, jealousy, deception, mistaken identity – and about an old man who takes a long time to realise that he has been thoroughly out-tricked. What follows are five other ways in which you can think about the play: story, revenge, England, 'sport' or public humiliation, and misusing the English language.

Story

There are two main plots. In the first, Falstaff pretends love to Mistress Ford and Mistress Page, hoping through them to get his hands on their husbands' money. But the Wives are virtuous and clever. They subject Falstaff to three crushing humiliations, and in so doing cure Master Ford of his obsessive jealousy. The second plot concerns the wooing of Anne Page. Her mother and father have different preferences for who should marry her, but when this plot merges with the Falstaff plot, their plans are foiled, and Anne marries her true love, Fenton. In a manic sub-plot, the Host of the Garter Inn is gulled, and throughout the play a variety of comic characters mangle the English language and contribute to the fun.

- Imagine you are one of the characters. Tell the story of the play as you experienced it.

A revenge play?

One way of thinking about *The Merry Wives of Windsor* is to see it as a revenge play, but with revenge as comedy, not as tragedy. The seemingly peaceful Windsor is riven by conflict. The very first words spoken are a demand for retribution, in Shallow's vehement declaration 'I will make a Star Chamber matter of it', and throughout the play many characters make similar threats. Nearly all engage in complicated intrigues and play-acting just as happens in revenge tragedy, but the result is to make the notion of revenge look ridiculous:

- Shallow wants action taken against Falstaff for stealing his deer. He doesn't get it!
- Slender wants redress on Falstaff and his followers for cheating him. He does not succeed.
- Pistol and Nim want revenge on Falstaff for sacking them. They reveal his plans to Ford.
- Doctor Caius wants revenge on Evans because of Anne Page. The proposed duel is prevented by the Host's trick.
- Doctor Caius and Evans want revenge on the Host for tricking them. They arrange for Germans to steal the Host's horses, and they invent a fictitious Duke who reserves rooms at the Garter.
- Master Ford wants revenge on Falstaff, who he thinks is seducing his wife. He finally gets revenge at Herne's Oak.
- Falstaff wants revenge on Ford for inadvertently humiliating him in the buck-basket and as the fat woman of Brentford. He fails spectacularly.

The Wives are the major avengers of the play. Affronted by Falstaff's misjudgement of their virtue, they humiliate him three times over.

- Turn to the List of characters on page 1. Which characters do not seem to want some kind of revenge on others? Suggest why not.

England

The Merry Wives of Windsor is remarkable in that it is Shakespeare's only play about ordinary people in a small English country town. It has been described as a 'citizen comedy', depicting everyday life familiar to Shakespeare and his Elizabethan contemporaries. It deals only with domestic affairs; there are no politics, no wars, no kings, no feuding barons. Windsor represents England in microcosm, and there is little or no sense of a wider world outside. What matters to Windsor's citizens is property, money, marriage, sport in all its forms, and of course, love – with all its absurdities.

Apart from the two visitors who have connections with the court (Falstaff and Fenton), the play is about the doings of the citizens, their wives, servants and hangers-on. There are the familiar professional members of the community: the doctor (here, a comic foreigner), the schoolteacher-parson (a Welshman), and the innkeeper. Mistress Quickly is the familiar figure of the small town gossip.

Although *The Merry Wives of Windsor* seems to be set in the fifteenth-century England of the history plays (Page refers to Fenton having 'kept company with the wild Prince and Poins' of the *King Henry IV* plays), it is much more obviously set in Shakespeare's own times. It is a comedy about the Elizabethan bourgeoisie, Shakespeare's own class. Ford and Page and their wives are concerned with the well-being of their homes and their local community. They are solid citizens, self-assured and well-off, but thrifty and proud. Securely middle class, they are wary of fortune hunters from the court or aristocracy. Ford's insanely jealous behaviour shows the high value Elizabethans put on marriage, and the ever-present threat of cuckoldry.

The play conveys a very powerful sense of place. Windsor is clearly established with its park, river, mead and castle. The court is in residence, possibly for Garter celebrations, and the town seems to be on holiday. William Page has a day off school, the Host is looking for sport in deceiving Evans and Caius, and the Wives engage in their trickery. Characters run greyhounds on the Cotswolds, go a-birding, cross fields and climb over styles, and get invited to drink a posset by a sea-coal fire.

'Sport': public humiliation

Productions of the play have often attempted to create a sense of 'Merry England', setting the play among innocent festivities such as morris-dancing, maypole-dances, and all kinds of traditional country sports, games, ceremonies and pageants. The recurring hunting imagery is used to illustrate theatre programmes with Elizabethan woodcuts of the pursuit of deer or other game. But the play is centrally concerned with a very different kind of 'sport': public rituals of shame and humiliation.

In Shakespeare's time, 'sport' could refer to customs known variously as 'charivari', 'skimmington', 'rough music', or 'riding'. These were all village or town activities in which someone who had violated a social norm was harassed and humiliated. For example, if a wife was believed to dominate her husband, or to beat him or be unfaithful to him, either the wife or husband might be tied, facing backwards, on a horse, and paraded round the village in a noisy procession that could include men wearing horns. The victim was raucously mocked in all kinds of ways – jeered at, insulted, and sometimes physically assaulted. Songs and proclamations, full of ridicule and word-play, would be directed at the offender.

Shakespeare seems to have had this notion of 'sport' in mind as he wrote *The Merry Wives of Windsor*. Ford promises Page 'you shall have sport', as he invites him to watch Mistress Ford being caught committing adultery with Falstaff. Page calls the planned humiliation of Falstaff at Herne's Oak a 'public sport', and after Falstaff is shamed, Mistress Page invites everyone home to 'laugh this sport o'er by a country fire'.

Falstaff's punishment resembles the 'sport' that was charivari. He has offended against social and domestic order by trying to seduce the wives, so he must be humiliated.

- He is covered by foul linen in the buck-basket and thrown into the Thames. His soul needs cleansing, just as does the dirty washing.
- He is beaten as the fat woman of Brentford: a fat female counterpart of himself.
- He faces public humiliation by Windsor citizens and children at Herne's Oak. The whole community is outraged by his behaviour. He is scorched with tapers, pinched by fairies, ridiculed for his appearance, and shown up as a fool.

Mangling the English language

The English language really takes a beating in *The Merry Wives of Windsor*. It seems as if Shakespeare wanted to show just how amusingly English can be mishandled. He draws attention to this in the way some characters talk about others as if they were enemies of the English language:

- Mistress Quickly says about Doctor Caius, 'here will be an old abusing of God's patience and the King's English'.
- Page says about Nim, 'here's a fellow frights English out of his wits'.
- The Host orders that Evans and Caius be disarmed to prevent the duel: 'Let them keep their limbs whole and hack our English.'
- Evans describes Pistol's language as 'affectations', and corrects Bardolph's malapropism of 'sentences' for 'senses', – 'Fie, what the ignorance is!'
- In the final scene, Falstaff declares that Evans 'makes fritters of English'; Ford doubts if Evans will ever speak 'good English'.

The world of the play

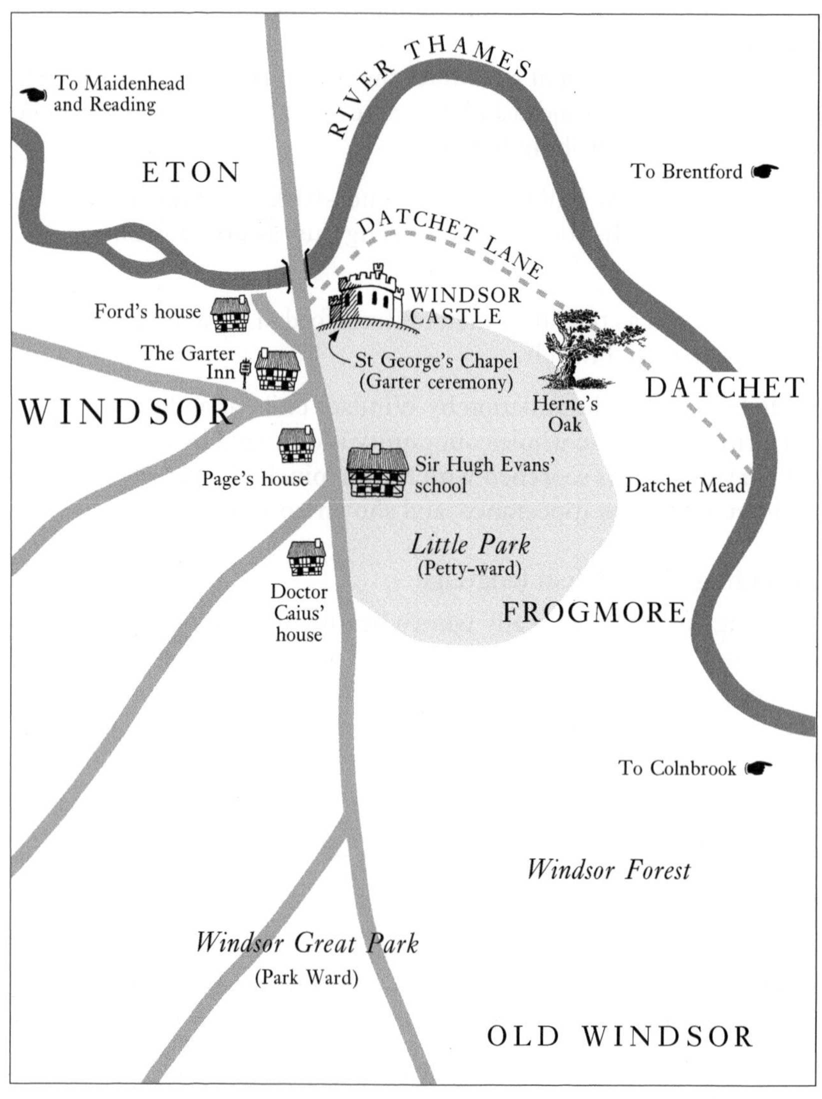

Shakespeare's imagined landscape of *The Merry Wives of Windsor*. Make your own enlarged copy of the map. Add illustrations or quotations to suggest what happens at some of the places shown.

Falstaff

Ever since Falstaff first stepped on stage over 400 years ago, he has enjoyed great success. Audiences took the fat knight to their hearts. Sometime around 1596–1598 Shakespeare wrote *King Henry IV Parts 1* and *2*, in which Falstaff appears as the dissolute companion of Prince Hal. For the young prince, Falstaff seems almost a father-figure, whose warmth and humour contrasts starkly with the coldness and disapproval of Hal's real father, King Henry IV.

But in those two history plays, Falstaff displays very obvious faults. He is totally egocentric, dedicated to pleasure, and ruled by his appetite for food, drink, sleep, women and money. Shakespeare shows him to be a thief, a liar, a drunkard and a swindling fraudster. He is a sponger and a coward who exploits others for his own advantage, and is always concerned to save his own skin. Devoid of morality, Falstaff is portrayed as self-seeking, unscrupulous and corrupt.

In spite of all his defects, Falstaff instantly became, and still remains, hugely popular. In the two history plays, he lives on his wits and has great resourcefulness and presence of mind. A relentless mocker of honour, he is a clear-sighted critic of power-seekers and the folly of society. He may be an opportunist, a lecher and a braggart, but he is also a rugged individualist full of wit and good humour. His brilliant command of the English language is at the root of his appeal.

In *King Henry IV Part 1*, Falstaff and Prince Hal enjoy the low life of the Boar's Head Tavern. They are involved in a robbery in which Falstaff behaves like a coward, running away. When he later boasts of his bravery, he is exposed by Hal as a liar. Falstaff goes reluctantly to war, and criticises honour and chivalry. He survives, and once again untruthfully proclaims his heroism, claiming to have killed the valiant Hotspur. In *Part 2*, Falstaff, oppressed by illness, is much less in the company of Hal, but plans to exploit his royal connections when the prince becomes king. He preys on Justice Shallow and Mistress Quickly, exploiting the friendship and hospitality they offer. Learning that Hal has become king, Falstaff rushes to London confident he can now become the most powerful person in England and do as he wishes. But Hal, now King Henry V, rejects him, 'I know thee not, old man', and Falstaff is carried off to prison.

Is Falstaff the same character in *The Merry Wives of Windsor* as he appears in the two history plays? He is still obviously an old reprobate and a predatory opportunist, hoping that his wild scheme of pretending to be in love with the Wives will enable him to get his hands on their money, and so restore his fortune. He remains a trickster, but in Windsor his tricks do not work because he grossly underestimates Mistress Ford and Mistress Page. Unlike the women in the *Henry IV* plays, he cannot twist the Wives around his little finger. They see through him instantly and plot their successful revenges.

In *Merry Wives*, Falstaff comes over as much more gullible and easily fooled than in the *Henry IV* plays. He is all too willing to believe what he is told, and is even ready to put on antlers and pretend to be a stag in the hope it will further his scheme to trick the Wives. Ironically, the would-be cuckold-maker ends up wearing the horns. Throughout the play, the Wives are more than a match for him, and he is the butt of their revenge plans, easily deceived and humiliated as he falls without suspicion into three successive traps: the buck-basket and the soaking in the Thames; being beaten as the fat woman of Brentford; and pinched, burned and mocked at Herne's Oak.

Unlike in the history plays, Falstaff appears as helpless as a child throughout *The Merry Wives of Windsor*. Shamed, exposed and ridiculed, he finishes up even more out of pocket than he began. As in the history plays, he is, like a scapegoat, rejected and driven out. But the difference is that in the comedy he is welcomed back, invited to join the Windsor community around Page's fireside to laugh over the events of the play.

Some critics have argued that Falstaff is a much diminished figure from how he appears in *King Henry IV Parts 1* and *2*. But his language still displays the witty inventiveness of those plays, full of vivid images and rich vocabulary. He may be dumped in the Thames, but he proves unsinkable, and uses self-mocking images to describe what would happen if the court heard of his humiliations:

> '... they would melt me out of my fat drop by drop, and liquor fishermen's boots with me. I warrant they would whip me with their fine wits till I were as crestfallen as a dried pear.' (Act 4 Scene 5, lines 77–9)

- As Falstaff progresses through the play he experiences all kinds of emotions. Make a list of all that happens to him from his first appearance in Act 1 Scene 1 to the final scene. Find a way of presenting his 'journey' through the play, for example, as a short play of your own devising, or a series of tableaux (frozen moments in the play), or as a diagram, graph or series of pictures or quotations.

Falstaff and the Wives at Herne's Oak (1789). Falstaff has long been a popular subject for artists. This painting by Robert Smirke (1752–1845) hangs in the picture gallery of the Royal Shakespeare Theatre, Stratford-upon-Avon. Compare it with other images of Falstaff on pages 33, 50, 84, 98, 118, 150, 171, 177.

The Merry Wives

In Elizabethan England, men were firmly in control. Husbands and fathers had almost absolute authority over the lives of their wives and daughters. Women's status and roles were subject to the tyranny of patriarchy (rule by men). Their rights were restricted legally, socially and economically. Legally, a married woman was little more than a slave: on marriage, all her possessions passed to her husband. Her property, her earnings, and even her children were under his absolute control. A husband was entitled to beat his wife as long as he did not endanger her life, and he could confine her for disobedience to his wishes, virtually imprisoning her. A father could dispose of his children in marriage as he saw fit. There was no legal obligation that he should take account of the wishes of his wife.

Religion was a powerful instrument to enforce the belief and practice of male superiority. The Elizabethan 'Homily of the State of Matrimony' was frequently read aloud in church. It ordered wives to obey their husbands, and instructed husbands that 'the woman is a frail vessel and thou art therefore made the ruler and head over her'. It saw the ideal woman as submissive, modest, virtuous – and inferior.

In a sermon preached before Queen Elizabeth I, Bishop Aylmer claimed:

> 'Women are of two sorts: some of them are wiser, better learned, discreeter, and more constant than a number of men; but another and worse sort of them are fond, foolish, wanton, flibbergibs, tattlers, triflers, wavering, witless, without council, feeble, careless, rash, proud, dainty, tale-bearers, eavesdroppers, rumour-raisers, evil-tongued, worse-minded, and in everyway doltified with the dregs of the devil's dunghill.'

It seems a very bleak picture, but the reality was often very different. Queen Elizabeth I very obviously possessed power and authority, but she was unmarried. Nonetheless, in her England, some husbands regarded their wives as equals, and in practice many wives got their own way by all kinds of methods. The stereotype of all Elizabethan males as patriarchal tyrants is far from the truth. In many families, male–female relationships were based on equality of respect and love. 'Companionate marriage' was a feature of a large number of Elizabethan homes: partnership and strong emotional ties.

The Merry Wives of Windsor, like all of Shakespeare's comedies, presents a picture of the condition of women in Elizabethan England very different from that of the stereotype of male dominance and oppression. Unlike most of Shakespeare's tragedies or histories, women characters have the major parts, and speak as many words as men. Mistress Alice Ford and Mistress Margaret Page are witty and intelligent, full of ingenuity and good humour. They more than hold their own with men in dialogue, and their actions powerfully influence or direct the development of plot. They use ridicule, not rancour, to conquer male jealousy, lust and greed.

The play shows the two women as independent spirits. They can obviously take care of themselves, and there is not much feeling that they are hedged in by their husbands' power, or feel that they should be silent and submissive. That they seem to enjoy a great deal of independence reflects a different aspect of Elizabethan society. Whilst most women had little or no legal power or autonomy, some did successfully achieve independence, managing their own estates or business. Many ran their own households with little or no interference from their husbands. It seems that the Wives manage their own affairs, and probably their husbands' too, holding the purse strings of the household. Falstaff greedily remarks about Mistress Ford, 'she has all the rule of her husband's purse', and about Mistress Page, 'She bears the purse too'.

Shakespeare seems to suggest the Wives have only one fault: for all their level-headedness they fail to see that Falstaff is really after their money, not their personal charms. But his depiction of Alice Ford and Margaret Page challenges and subverts the conventional negative portrayal of Elizabethan women as weak, submissive and pliable. The Wives defy patriarchal control and flourish as they enjoy power and freedom in Windsor. They make Falstaff an object of ridicule, teach Ford a lesson in love, and Meg Page plots against her husband's plan for their daughter's marriage (but both husband and wife lose out to true love as Anne marries Fenton).

Nonetheless, disturbing aspects of the condition of Elizabethan women are reflected in the play. Anne is regarded by her father as a possession he can give in marriage to whoever he chooses. Falstaff, disguised as an old woman (mother Pratt or the witch of Brentford), is beaten 'all the colours of the rainbow' by Ford, and Mistress Quickly (falsely) reports that Ford has also beaten his wife 'black and blue'. Everyone in the play seems to take it for granted that such violence against women is acceptable.

Why 'merry'?

Mistress Ford and Mistress Page may be past the 'holiday time' of their beauty, but they are clearly young at heart, fun-loving and full of delighted energy. But Elizabethans watching the play would know that 'merry' meant more than enjoying practical jokes. In Shakespeare's time, 'merry' also had the meaning of sexual playing around. But that is a meaning that the Wives directly deny, when Mistress Page declares, 'Wives may be merry and yet honest too.'

The Wives may be broad-spoken and enjoy the bawdy, but they are both faithful to their husbands, and their reputations matter to them. They prove to be the protectors of Windsor's traditional values. They are indignant and affronted by Falstaff's assumption that he can easily seduce them: 'What doth he think of us?' explodes an outraged Mistress Ford. Indignant at his low estimate of their morals and their intelligence, they vow revenge, and extract it in full measure. They prove to be enterprising plotters who use their powers of invention to teach Falstaff a humiliating lesson. He painfully learns that they are not the easily available women he takes them to be, that they will not deceive their husbands, and that their marriages are secure. The jealous Ford learns the same lesson.

The play uses much imagery of hunting, but it is the two women who turn into hunters and catch the stag, Falstaff. Nonetheless, their good-hearted nature is evident in their generous response at the play's end, as Mistress Page invites Falstaff home to supper to laugh over the day's absurdities with all the Windsor citizens.

A Dutch visitor to England wrote in 1575:

'Wives in England … are not kept so strictly as they are in Spain or elsewhere. They go to the market to buy what they like best to eat. They are well dressed, fond of taking it easy, and commonly leave the care of household matters and drudgery to their servants. They sit before their doors, decked out in fine clothes, in order to see and be seen by the passers-by … their time they employ in walking and riding, in playing at cards or otherwise, in visiting their friends and keeping company, conversing with their equals (whom they term gossips) and their neighbours, and making merry with them at child-births, christenings, churchings and funerals … England is called the Paradise of married women.'

Falstaff fails to see the Merry Wives' true intentions for him. How does this picture convey that Mistress Page and Mistress Ford are only playing up to Falstaff?

Characters

Falstaff and the Wives are discussed on pages 165–171. Many of the other characters are traditional dramatic types. Their acting style is suggested by their role: the jealous husband (Ford), the foolish magistrate (Shallow), the courtly lover (Fenton), the hapless lover (Slender), the braggart (Pistol), the garrulous woman (Mistress Quickly), the ridiculous foreigner (Doctor Caius), and the simpleton (Peter Simple). But Shakespeare gives each character a distinctive voice or verbal tic which creates a unique personality and stage presence. Many have odd styles of speech which commit hilarious violence on the Queen's English. Their misuse of language makes them sound as if they have stepped out of a Ben Jonson play or from the sub-plot of a novel by Charles Dickens. They have been called 'grotesques', 'caricatures', 'obsessives' and 'eccentrics', but in performance actors can make them convincingly human.

Mistress Quickly

In *King Henry IV Parts 1* and *2*, Mistress Quickly is Hostess of the Boar's Head Tavern in London's Eastcheap, where she is grossly exploited by Falstaff. In *The Merry Wives of Windsor*, she is Doctor Caius' housekeeper (but does not know Falstaff), and has the same characteristics as in the history plays. She is kind-hearted, garrulous and often uses malapropisms (mistaking one word for another): 'allicholy' for melancholy, 'canaries' for quandaries, 'speciously' for specially, and so on. Like many other characters, she is given to repetition: 'Coach after coach, letter after letter, gift after gift'.

Mistress Quickly is a busybody and trickster, full of irrepressible energy. The Wives see her as a valuable go-between in their plot against Falstaff, but her habit of wandering off the point, flitting from one thought to another, prompts him to protest, 'Be brief, my good she-Mercury.' She mistakes Evans' Latin lesson with William Page as riddled with sexual meaning. When Evans asks William about the 'genitive case', and the boy replies '*Genitivo, horum, harum, horum*', she thinks she hears of prostitution, and explodes: 'Vengeance of Jenny's case! Fie on her! Never name her, child, if she be a whore.'

Sir Hugh Evans

Sir Hugh Evans is Windsor's schoolmaster and clergyman, proud of his learning, and aware of his position as a scholar among the townsfolk. He is very pedantic, given to correcting other characters' speech. A little cowardly, he is clearly apprehensive as he waits for Doctor Caius to appear for the duel, singing to himself to keep his spirits up. And he is very Welsh! Shakespeare seems to have enjoyed exaggerating his accent to make him the parody of the stage Welshman with distinctive pronunciation (for example, using 'p' for 'b' as in 'prain' for brain) and curious syntax: 'Ay, and her father is make her a petter penny.'

Doctor Caius

Windsor's rich foreign doctor has important connections at court. Perhaps courtiers are his patients. He is very quick-tempered, typically using 'By gar' (By God) to express his angry feelings. Shakespeare makes him exaggeratedly French, inviting Elizabethans to laugh at him (making fun of foreigners was a popular sport). Caius is the butt of jokes of other characters, and is tricked into nearly marrying a boy rather than Anne Page. Mistress Quickly prepares the audience for his irascibility and strange language: 'here will be an old abusing of God's patience and the King's English'. True to form, Caius mixes French and English, 'Pray you go and vetch me in my closet *une boite en vert* – a box, a green-a box.' Shakespeare adds to the sense of the ridiculous by having Caius unknowingly speak very coarsely as he proposes to join Page and Evans, 'I shall make-a the turd.'

The Host

The Host of the Garter Inn is a larger-than-life character. Bluff, outgoing and friendly, he seems full of good humour, calling everyone 'Bully', and using a jovial, blustering style of speech, rich in colourful exaggeration. Until he learns that his horses have been stolen, and that he has been tricked about the visiting duke, he seems almost the model of the merry, mischievous innkeeper as he plays his trick on Evans and Caius to prevent them duelling. He often speaks in short, clipped phrases, giving an urgency and portentousness to his language: 'What says my bully rook? Speak scholarly and wisely … Discard, bully Hercules, cashier. Let them wag; trot, trot … Thou'rt an emperor: Caesar, Kaiser, and Pheazar.'

Justice Shallow

Many people believe that Shallow is Shakespeare's mocking caricature of the real-life Sir Thomas Lucy. The legend goes that Shakespeare poached the deer in Sir Thomas' park at Charlecote, close to Stratford-upon-Avon. To avoid arrest, he left Stratford and journeyed to London. At Act 1 Scene 1, lines 12–13, the audience learns that Shallow has a 'dozen white luces' (pike) in his coat of arms. The Lucy family had only three silver pike on their coat of arms, so the exaggeration shows Shallow as vain and very conscious of his social position. Over eighty years old, he claims to have been a great fighter in his youth.

Shallow had appeared in *King Henry IV Part 2* as a foolish and boastful old country magistrate who is deceived by Falstaff and cheated out of £1000. He is the same character in *Merry Wives*: repetitive, rambling, boastful about his youthful exploits (probably fictitious) and keen to emphasise his social status. The impression of a foolish old man, concerned with what he sees as his own high status is emphasised in his habit of repeating what he says: 'He hath wronged me, indeed he hath, at a word he hath. Believe me. Robert Shallow, Esquire, saith he is wronged.'

Slender

Slender is a simple country gentleman, quite out of his depth in Windsor. He gets his pocket picked by Falstaff's followers, and is almost inarticulate and full of embarrassment as Anne Page's wooer. His bashfulness is no match for her directness. He knows no Latin, can talk only of greyhounds and bears (about which he probably knows little), and he is a remarkably incompetent lover, wishing that he had his *Songs and Sonnets* to help him woo. Like most other characters, he malaprops: 'All his successors gone before him hath done't, and all his ancestors that come after him may.' There is a strong hint of femininity in his repeated use of 'la', and like a child he excuses himself, 'I bruised my shin the other day with playing at sword and dagger with a master of fence.'

But although he may be a total nonentity, on stage, Slender is a great comic character. He can engage the sympathies of the audience, especially in Act 3 Scene 1, where his only contribution is the occasional repetition of 'O sweet Anne Page!', and in the final scene where he expresses total confusion at having run off with a boy and nearly marrying him in mistake for Anne.

Fenton and Anne Page

Fenton and Anne Page seem to have stepped out of a different play. They are quite unlike the eccentric characters who populate *The Merry Wives of Windsor*. Uncomplicated, young, intelligent and very much in love, their sanity contrasts sharply with the mayhem that surrounds them. Fenton is a dashing young courtier, said to have kept company with Prince Hal and Poins (but he does not appear in the *Henry IV* plays). As a result of his wild adventures he is penniless. His original purpose in wooing Anne was that of a fortune hunter: to get his hands on her father's money. But he has fallen in love with her and wants Anne only for herself.

Fenton and Falstaff make a striking contrast: both men are high status, having connections with the court, and both have squandered their money. Both learn from their pursuit of Windsor citizens' wealth, but Falstaff's is a painful lesson, whilst Fenton learns to love, and comes to see Anne as 'of more value/Than stamps in gold'.

Anne has comparatively little to say, but clearly possesses practical common sense and intelligence. She may be sweet and innocent, but she displays an engaging country directness as she declares her view on marrying Slender, 'Alas, I had rather be set quick i'th'earth,/And bowled to death with turnips.'

Pistol, Nim and Bardolph

Pistol, Nim and Bardolph are Falstaff's followers or hangers-on. They are the same disreputable characters as they were in *King Henry V* (where Nim is spelled Nym) and in the *King Henry IV* plays (in which Nim does not appear), landless and homeless soldiers whose real interest in war is bragging about their bravery, but who avoid danger, and profit from whatever they can steal or loot.

Pistol is the braggart from *King Henry IV Part 2*, the *miles gloriosus* of Italian comedies, a coward who pretends to be brave. He swaggers and boasts, and his exaggerated language is full of misquotations. He tries to speak like a hero of melodrama, using poetic, dramatic speech. But as he wrenches lines out of plays, he produces only inconsequential rant. His concern to give himself airs is evident (Act 2 Scene 2, lines 108–10) in the inflated image of a sea battle he uses as he proposes to pursue Mistress Quickly:

> 'This punk is one of Cupid's carriers.
> Clap on more sails; pursue; up with your fights;
> Give fire; she is my prize, or ocean whelm them all!'

Nim is another braggart, a sort of poor man's Pistol, who tries to appear ominously aggressive. He is fixated on the word 'humour', using it in almost every sentence he speaks, as in his warning to Ford to suspect Mistress Ford:

> 'And this is true. I like not the humour of lying. He hath wronged me in some humours. I should have borne the humoured letter to her … Adieu. I love not the humour of bread and cheese. Adieu.'
>
> (Act 2 Scene 1, lines 107–13)

Bardolph had appeared in *Henry IV Parts 1* and *2*, in which his nose, swollen and inflamed by drink, was the butt for Falstaff's jokes. That joking continues in *Merry Wives*, his red nose continues to be mocked. Like other characters, he mangles words and uses malapropism: 'I say the gentleman had drunk himself out of his five sentences.' Bardolph's part in the play seems to be to change from Falstaff's follower to the tapster (barman) at the Garter Inn.

Ford and Page

Master George Page trusts his wife, and seems remarkably ordinary (but he does wish to choose his daughter's husband, against Anne's and his wife's wishes). In stark contrast, Master Frank Ford is an insanely jealous husband. He may be a stock character of comedy, but his individuality shines through brilliantly in performance. He evokes very mixed responses from audiences, ranging from laughter at his ridiculously intense suspicion and behaviour, to sympathy for his tortured feelings and eventual reconciliation and self-awareness.

Ford is a sort of private eye, an investigator who aims to catch his wife and Falstaff together, cuckolding him. He is utterly convinced he knows the truth, but he keeps getting caught in his own traps, failing to find Falstaff and unwittingly aiding the fat knight's escape. His emotions swing violently, one moment triumphant, thinking he has succeeded in trapping Falstaff, the next utterly frustrated at failing to find him. What he learns from Falstaff makes him positively incandescent, exploding in outbursts of mixed feelings! The fact that the audience always knows what is really going on adds to the hilarity.

Ford is obsessed with thoughts of cuckoldry. Images of horns (the symbol of the deceived husband) pervade his language. Some critics have seen Ford as like Othello, so consumed with jealousy, and so anguished by thoughts of revenge, that it is impossible for him to see or think clearly. His fixation, the violence of his emotions, and his manic behaviour evoke audience laughter, but his intentions have a chilling realism as he threatens revenge on Falstaff, and contemplates torturing his wife, revealing Mistress Page as another adultress, and mocking his friend and neighbour George Page. His language, like Othello's in the madness of suspicion, is fragmentary and jumpy in its confused syntax and tortured images. On hearing the word 'buck' (used about the washing in the buck-basket, but which could also mean a rutting stag), his sexual fixations explode in almost incoherent repetition:

> 'Buck? I would I could wash myself of the buck! Buck, buck, buck! Ay, buck! I warrant you, buck.'
>
> (Act 3 Scene 3, lines 122–3)

Ford disguises himself as Master Brook to find out just what is going on between Falstaff and Mistress Ford. But what Falstaff tells him confirms all Ford's suspicions of his wife, and causes him excruciating mental agony!

The language of the play

Imagery

Imagery is the use of emotionally charged words and phrases which can conjure up vivid pictures in the imagination. Such images intensify the dramatic and emotional impact of the play and help create its distinctive atmosphere and themes. The domestic life of Windsor is echoed and created in all kinds of everyday images: 'toasted cheese', 'fritters', 'rain potatoes', 'butcher's offal', 'I'll have my brains ta'en out and buttered', and so on.

The English countryside is evoked through images of nature and animals. Fenton 'smells April and May'; Falstaff talks of his childhood when he 'plucked geese, played truant, and whipped top'; the Wives intend to teach Falstaff 'to know turtles from jays' (love-birds from gaudy scavengers). Imagery of hunting recurs, for example, Ford expresses his hope to discover Falstaff as 'unkennel the fox'. The hunting images reflect Falstaff's pursuit of the Wives, and how he in turn becomes hunted. They also express the play's obsession with cuckoldry, in images of horns, bucks, rut-time.

Imagery contributes to the creation of character, most obviously in emphasising Falstaff's huge size. He is variously described as 'a hodge pudding', 'a puffed man', 'this gross watery pumpkin'. Images of oil, fat and grease add to the audience's impression of Falstaff as bloated and sweating. Mistress Ford wonders at 'this whale, with so many tuns of oil in his belly'. Falstaff describes himself in the buck-basket as 'half stewed in grease like a Dutch dish', and thinks how he will be mocked by the court: 'they would melt me out of my fat drop by drop, and liquor fishermen's boots with me'.

Imagery based on Elizabethans' familiarity with scripture also recurs, as in 'the story of the prodigal', 'a legion of angels', 'a Cain-coloured beard', 'a Herod of Jewry', 'Goliath with a weaver's beam', 'all Eve's daughters', and so on. Greek mythology provides a notable sexual image used by several characters: that of Actaeon, who saw Diana bathing naked, and was turned into a stag and then pursued to destruction by his own hounds. Elsewhere, Falstaff displays his knowledge of the classical world of Greece and Rome with other sexually potent images of Jove and Europa, Jupiter and Leda.

All Shakespeare's imagery uses metaphor or simile. A simile compares one thing to another using 'like' ('vanish like hailstones', 'like a horseshoe – hissing hot') or 'as' ('as poor as Job', 'as wicked as his wife'). A metaphor is also a comparison. It does not use 'like' or 'as' but suggests that two dissimilar things are actually the same. For example, Pistol describes Mistress Page looking at Falstaff as 'Then did the sun on dunghill shine.' Falstaff describes Pistol's 'cat-a-mountain looks', and, relishing the thought that his pursuit of the Wives will make him rich, uses imagery drawn from Elizabethan voyages of discovery and exploitation: 'Sail like my pinnace to these golden shores', 'She is a region in Guiana, all gold and bounty', 'They shall be my East and West Indies, and I will trade to them both.'

- Falstaff's language is rich in imagery. Turn to some scenes in which he appears and identify the images he uses. Suggest how they add to the dramatic appeal of the scene, for example, in creating atmosphere or conveying a sense of character or theme.

Language is character

Shakespeare gives each character a distinctive voice or odd, amusing style of speech which creates a unique personality and stage presence. Many characters use malapropisms, mistaking one word for another (as in Mistress Quickly's 'fartuous' for 'virtuous'). See pages 172–7 for examples of how language creates character.

Insults

The play is full of insults, or language that could be used as insults. Collect as many as you can, divide them into those used about Falstaff and those used about other characters. Then work with a partner speaking the insults to each other accompanying each with a suitable gesture. Here are just a few to start you off:

'Banbury cheese!'
'Froth and scum'
'Flemish drunkard'
'monsieur Mockwater'
'Let vultures gripe thy guts'
'his guts are made of puddings'
'scurvy, cogging companion'
'mountain of mummy'
'you witch'
'you rag'

'latten bilbo!'
'brazen-face'
'intolerable entrails'
'hodge pudding'
'Hungarian wight'
'great lubberly boy'
'bag of flax'
'you polecat'
'you runnion'
'you baggage'

Lists

One of Shakespeare's favourite methods with language is to accumulate words or phrases rather like a list. He knew that 'piling up' item on item, incident on incident, could intensify description, atmosphere, character and dramatic effect. The play is rich in lists, for example, as Falstaff dismisses Pistol and Nim: 'Rogues, hence, avaunt! Vanish like hailstones, go! / Trudge, plod away o'th'hoof, seek shelter, pack!' (Act 1 Scene 3, lines 62–3).

Mistress Quickly describes how she serves Doctor Caius: 'I keep his house, and I wash, wring, brew, bake, scour, dress meat and drink, make the beds, and do all myself –' (Act 1 Scene 4, lines 81–3).

Ford, in the torment of jealousy, draws on anti-foreigner stereotypes as he lists all he would rather trust than his wife: 'I will rather trust a Fleming with my butter, Parson Hugh the Welshman with my cheese, an Irishman with my aquavitae bottle, or a thief to walk my ambling gelding, than my wife with herself.' (Act 2 Scene 2, lines 236–9).

Moments later Ford lists the actions he intends: 'I will prevent this, detect my wife, be revenged on Falstaff, and laugh at Page.' (Act 2 Scene 2, lines 242–3).

- Lists offer imaginative opportunities for acting out. Choose one of the lists above (or one of your own choice from elsewhere in the play). Speak it in a style you think suitable, then work with others to perform the list in some way.

Verse and prose

It seems that Shakespeare decided to write a prose comedy. Only about twelve per cent of *The Merry Wives of Windsor* is in verse, less than in any other Shakespeare play. The play-writing convention of the time was that high-status characters spoke in verse, and that prose was used for comedy or by low-status characters. The verse is mainly associated with Fenton. He uses it exclusively, and when characters speak to him they also usually speak in verse. Falstaff (the other high-status character) nearly always uses prose, probably because Shakespeare judged him 'comic'. Elsewhere, Ford's apology to his wife and the plot to trick Falstaff at Herne's Oak are in verse (Act 4 Scene 4), perhaps because they are 'serious' moments. Pistol bombastically declaims in verse as he puts on an act as a tragic hero, and the Queen of the Fairies and her attendants use verse in the masque at Herne's Oak.

Repetition

Repeated words, phrases, rhythms and sounds add to the dramatic force of the play. Repetition helps create character. Nim obsessively repeats 'humour', the Host 'bully', Caius 'By gar', and Shallow is much given to repeating his own expressions: 'He's a good dog and a fair dog ... He is good and fair.' Ford is tormented by the thought of his wife's infidelity: 'Fie, fie, fie! Cuckold, cuckold, cuckold!' His sexual obsessions are evident in his fevered repetition of the word 'buck' (see pages 86, 177), and in the abrupt rhythms of his short sentences as he remonstrates with himself after hearing how he failed to catch Falstaff: 'Hum! Ha! Is this a vision? Is this a dream? Do I sleep? Master Ford, awake! Awake, Master Ford!' (Act 3 Scene 5, lines 110–11).

The prose of the play is highly patterned. Soliloquies and speeches include repeated words or phrases which structure the language. Such structures can be seen in Falstaff's invocation at Herne's Oak as he thinks of aphrodisiacs 'Let the ... let it ... let there ...' (see page 147); in Ford's agonised thoughts after his first meeting with Falstaff ('My bed shall be abused, my coffers ransacked, my reputation gnawn at'); and in Falstaff's letter to the Wives which can be set out as:

'You are not young, no more am I.
Go to, then, there's sympathy.
You are merry, so am I.
Ha, ha, then, there's more sympathy.
You love sack, and so do I.
Would you desire better sympathy?' (Act 2 Scene 1, lines 4–7)

- Turn to one of Falstaff's or Ford's soliloquies, and speak it to a partner, trying to bring out the repeated rhythms within it.

Familiar phrases

Many phrases from the play have become familiar expressions: 'What the dickens', 'the world's mine oyster', 'as good luck would have it', 'beaten black and blue', 'all the colours of the rainbow', 'a man of my kidney', 'speaks small like a woman', 'we burn daylight', 'in despite of the teeth of all rhyme and reason'.

- Use these expressions (and any others you find) in a short story of your own invention.

Shakespeare finds his story

Why did Shakespeare write *The Merry Wives of Windsor*? There is a popular legend that Queen Elizabeth I so much enjoyed seeing Falstaff in the *Henry IV* plays that she commanded Shakespeare to write a play about Falstaff in love – and to write it within fourteen days! It's an attractive story, but is probably untrue. The claim was made a hundred years after the play was first performed, and there is no documentary evidence for it.

What is much more likely is that, just as with all his plays, Shakespeare's imagination was fired by stories he had read. Those tales contained elements which turn up in *The Merry Wives of Windsor*: jealous and cuckolded husbands; a man who sends the same love letter to several women who decide to punish him; lovers who have narrow escapes and unknowingly confide in the husbands; parents who prefer rival suitors for their daughter.

The buck-basket and Master Brook: An Italian collection of stories, *Il Pecorone* (c.1558), which also gave Shakespeare the main plot of *The Merchant of Venice*, contains the tale of a student who wants to seduce a woman. He asks his professor how he should set about the seduction. What neither men know is that the woman is the professor's wife. The student visits the wife, but hearing the husband approaching, hides underneath the laundry. The next day he visits the professor and tells him how he escaped. On a second occasion, the professor runs his sword through the laundry, and is regarded as mad by his friends.

The Old Woman of Brentford: an English collection of stories, *Riche his Farewell to the Military Profession* (1581), which gave Shakespeare much of the plot of *Twelfth Night*, tells the story of a wife who tricks a former lover, a doctor, into carrying out of her house a bag in which is concealed another lover. The doctor thinks the woman is in the bag, but is amazed to see a face with a long beard!

Falstaff's love letters: Shakespeare probably knew a story in a book by William Painter called *The Palace of Pleasure* (1566). It tells of a student who sent identical love letters to three women. They compare notes and decide to punish him.

Tormenting Falstaff: John Lyly's *Endimion* (c.1588) has a character pinched by fairies who cry 'Pinch him, pinch him, black and blue'.

The Anne Page sub-plot: the Roman playwright Plautus (c.254–184 BC, who Shakespeare studied at school), dramatised a somewhat similar story of a father and mother who prefer different suitors for their daughter.

Popular culture also probably contributed to Shakespeare's imagination as he wrote *Merry Wives*. Elizabethans loved the 'merry tales' they found in the widely read jest-books of the time. Such tales were typically about trickery, often of women tricking men. Foreigners were ridiculed, and Welshmen mocked for their fondness for toasted cheese. Other popular publications were 'cony-catching' pamphlets, which told how criminals cheated, for example, by pretending to love a serving maid to gain access to a house.

A painting by David Scott (1840) of Queen Elizabeth I watching a performance of *The Merry Wives of Windsor* at the Globe Theatre. It is all fictitious, but join in the fun! Imagine you were present at the performance for the queen. Write your account of what happened.

Critics' forum

'Falstaff could not love but by ceasing to be Falstaff. He could only counterfeit love, and his professions could be prompted, not by the hope of pleasure, but of money.'
Samuel Johnson, 1773

'No doubt *The Merry Wives of Windsor* is a very amusing play, with a great deal of humour, character and nature in it: but we should have liked it much better, if anyone else had been the hero of it, instead of Falstaff ... Falstaff is not the man he was in the two parts of *Henry IV*. His wit and eloquence have left him. Instead of making a butt of others, he is made a butt of by them. Neither is there a single particle of love in him to excuse his follies: he is merely a designing, bare-faced knave, and an unsuccessful one.'
William Hazlitt, 1817

'In the first act alone of *The Merry Wives of Windsor* there is more life and movement than in all German literature.'
Friedrich Engels writing to Karl Marx, 1873

'Falstaff ... baffled, duped, treated like dirty linen, beaten, burnt, pricked, mocked, insulted, and, worst of all, repentant and didactic. It is horrible.'
A C Bradley, 1909

'After *The Comedy of Errors* it is Shakespeare's most heartless farce. And this is too bad, since it is his only citizen play, his one local and contemporary piece. In another mood he might have made much of Ford and Page, and of their wives who to our loss are here so coarse-grained, so monotonous and broad-hipped in their comic dialect.'
Mark van Doren, 1939

'Falstaff is gulled as expected, but so, to their own amazement, are four of the contrivers of the Herne the Hunter comedy, Page and his wife, Caius and Slender. Like *Hamlet*, to which it is close in date, *The Merry Wives of Windsor* is filled with affirmations of the power of illusion. It reminds the theatre audience that life is constantly discovering within itself bewildering conjunctions with the drama, that at times the world cannot easily be distinguished from the stage.'
Anne Righter, 1962

'You can sometimes galvanise a corpse – no one can breathe life into a waxworks dummy. *The Merry Wives of Windsor* should be allowed to remain in the basement as the only really botched job in Shakespeare's repertoire.'
Alan Brien, 1964

'*The Merry Wives* is the only play which deals with the new middle class and its relationship with the men from the court. Falstaff, whose life has been spent on the fringes of the court, comes into contact with this other class and fails to understand it. Taken in by the forthright humour of the merry wives themselves, he cannot see that they possess not only intelligence but virtue. The play, therefore, has a central conflict between two different levels of society. Yet, just as Falstaff has to learn the true nature of Mistress Page and Mistress Ford, so the Page family in their turn have to learn the true nature of the other courtier in the play, Master Fenton.'
Terry Hands, 1968

'*The Merry Wives* is not a light-hearted mid-summer romp, or a springtime celebration, but rather a record of the transition from fall to winter – an effort to put the house in order, to become reconciled to the passing of fertility from the old to the young. Just beyond the frivolity of the play's pranks and the "innocent" revenge of its night-wandering spirits lie the gravity and earnestness of a sober new year.'
Jeanne Addison Roberts, 1979

'The setting is bourgeois, settled, prosperous and imbued with a moral complacency ... The major themes of the play are the cornerstones of bourgeois life: possession of property, possession of women, and fear of theft ... The Host is jealous and possessive about his property; Caius is jealous and possessive about his house and closets; Ford is jealous and possessive about his wife; Page is jealous and possessive about his daughter, whom he sees as property to be disposed of as he chooses; Caius, Evans and Slender see Anne the same way (no wonder she speaks so little in the play). Even Fenton confesses to her that his original intention in courting her was to gain control of her wealth.'
Marilyn French, 1981

'The most important fact about Windsor is conflict ... In the range and variety of conflicts and attempted resolutions, the play provides a casebook of conflict in an Elizabethan town. Local and national law, the private code of the duel, trickery, neighbourly intervention, and public humiliation are all part of the social repertory of the citizens of Windsor.'
Edward Berry, 2001

Staging *The Merry Wives of Windsor*

The play was first performed sometime between 1597 and 1601. Some scholars believe it was staged at the Garter feast in Whitehall before Queen Elizabeth I and her court on St George's Day, 23 April 1597 (see page 182). Others believe the first performance was at the Globe Theatre on London's Bankside. No one can be really sure about the first performance, but it is known that the play was performed in 1604 at the court of King James I, and for his son Charles I in 1638.

The Puritans closed the theatres from 1642 to 1660, but when they reopened *The Merry Wives of Windsor* was one of the first plays to be performed. The diarist Samuel Pepys did not think highly of the play in performance. He enjoyed Slender and Caius but disliked everything else. It seems that Restoration audiences of the time thought the play 'rustic' and unsophisticated, perhaps because country virtue (the Wives) triumphed over the court (Falstaff).

In 1702, John Dennis rewrote the play as *The Comical Gallant or the Amours of Sir John Falstaff*. But Dennis' version was a failure, and a revival of Shakespeare's play in 1721 enjoyed great success, and it has been a firm favourite with audiences ever since, as popular in America and Germany as in England. Part of its appeal for actors and audiences alike is that it abounds in a variety of parts that give many opportunities for comic business.

The Merry Wives of Windsor has inspired numerous musical adaptations, most notably Verdi's opera *Falstaff* (1893), and Ralph Vaughan Williams' *Sir John in Love* (1929).

The play seems to be set in the fifteenth-century England of the history plays (see page 162). However, it is clearly set in Shakespeare's own times, and most productions have given the play an Elizabethan setting with half-timbered houses and male characters dressed in costumes of the 1590s. Other versions have included:

- a 'wintry' production (1911) with the stage covered in four inches of salt to represent snow, and characters in mufflers and mittens.
- a modern dress production (1929) with Anne Page riding pillion on Fenton's motor-bike.
- a Russian production (1957) with a 'merry fair' in the intervals at which actors and audience mingled.

This Royal Shakespeare Company production (1985) was set in the 1950s. The Wives made their first appearance under hair driers in a beauty parlour.

Staging your production

- Imagine a sponsor is willing to pay all costs if you can persuade her your proposed production of *The Merry Wives of Windsor* is worthwhile. Present your case!
- Design a poster to advertise your production. You might wish to use images of the buck-basket, Elizabethan Windsor, and so on.
- Make your suggestion of a time, other than the Elizabethan period, in which the play might be set. How would the Wives appear in that production?

William Shakespeare 1564–1616

1564 Born Stratford-upon-Avon, eldest son of John and Mary Shakespeare.
1582 Marries Anne Hathaway of Shottery, near Stratford.
1583 Daughter, Susanna, born.
1585 Twins, son and daughter, Hamnet and Judith, born.
1592 First mention of Shakespeare in London. Robert Greene, another playwright, described Shakespeare as 'an upstart crow beautified with our feathers ...'. Greene seems to have been jealous of Shakespeare. He mocked Shakespeare's name, calling him 'the only Shake-scene in a country' (presumably because Shakespeare was writing successful plays).
1595 A shareholder in 'The Lord Chamberlain's Men', an acting company that became extremely popular.
1596 Son Hamnet dies, aged eleven.
Father, John, granted arms (acknowledged as a gentleman).
1597 Buys New Place, the grandest house in Stratford.
1598 Acts in Ben Jonson's *Every Man in His Humour*.
1599 Globe Theatre opens on Bankside. Performances in the open air.
1601 Father, John, dies.
1603 James I grants Shakespeare's company a royal patent: 'The Lord Chamberlain's Men' became 'The King's Men' and played about twelve performances each year at court.
1607 Daughter, Susanna, marries Dr John Hall.
1608 Mother, Mary, dies.
1609 'The King's Men' begin performing indoors at Blackfriars Theatre.
1610 Probably returned from London to live in Stratford.
1616 Daughter, Judith, marries Thomas Quiney.
Dies. Buried in Holy Trinity Church, Stratford-upon-Avon.

The plays and poems

(no one knows exactly when he wrote each play)

1589–1595 *The Two Gentlemen of Verona*, *The Taming of the Shrew*, *First, Second and Third Parts of King Henry VI*, *Titus Andronicus*, *King Richard III*, *The Comedy of Errors*, *Love's Labour's Lost*, *A Midsummer Night's Dream*, *Romeo and Juliet*, *King Richard II* (and the long poems *Venus and Adonis* and *The Rape of Lucrece*).

1596–1599 *King John*, *The Merchant of Venice*, *First and Second Parts of King Henry IV*, *The Merry Wives of Windsor*, *Much Ado About Nothing*, *King Henry V*, *Julius Caesar* (and probably the *Sonnets*).

1600–1605 *As You Like It*, *Hamlet*, *Twelfth Night*, *Troilus and Cressida*, *Measure for Measure*, *Othello*, *All's Well That Ends Well*, *Timon of Athens*, *King Lear*.

1606–1611 *Macbeth*, *Antony and Cleopatra*, *Pericles*, *Coriolanus*, *The Winter's Tale*, *Cymbeline*, *The Tempest*.

1613 *King Henry VIII*, *The Two Noble Kinsmen* (both probably with John Fletcher).

1623 Shakespeare's plays published as a collection (now called the First Folio).